Importance of English Language f

Deepesh Kumar Thakur

Importance of English Language for Professional& Technical Education

Exposure to the actual work environment and including the application

LAP LAMBERT Academic Publishing

Impressum/Imprint (nur für Deutschland/only for Germany)
Bibliografische Information der Deutschen Nationalbibliothek: Die Deutsche Nationalbibliothek verzeichnet diese Publikation in der Deutschen Nationalbibliografie; detaillierte bibliografische Daten sind im Internet über http://dnb.d-nb.de abrufbar.
Alle in diesem Buch genannten Marken und Produktnamen unterliegen warenzeichen-, marken- oder patentrechtlichem Schutz bzw. sind Warenzeichen oder eingetragene Warenzeichen der jeweiligen Inhaber. Die Wiedergabe von Marken, Produktnamen, Gebrauchsnamen, Handelsnamen, Warenbezeichnungen u.s.w. in diesem Werk berechtigt auch ohne besondere Kennzeichnung nicht zu der Annahme, dass solche Namen im Sinne der Warenzeichen- und Markenschutzgesetzgebung als frei zu betrachten wären und daher von jedermann benutzt werden dürften.

Coverbild: www.ingimage.com

Verlag: LAP LAMBERT Academic Publishing GmbH & Co. KG
Heinrich-Böcking-Str. 6-8, 66121 Saarbrücken, Deutschland
Telefon +49 681 3720-310, Telefax +49 681 3720-3109
Email: info@lap-publishing.com

Approved by: Muzaffarpur,Baba Saheb BhimRAo Ambedkar Bihar University,Bihar,INDIA,Dissertation,2004-2006

Herstellung in Deutschland (siehe letzte Seite)
ISBN: 978-3-659-18858-9

Imprint (only for USA, GB)
Bibliographic information published by the Deutsche Nationalbibliothek: The Deutsche Nationalbibliothek lists this publication in the Deutsche Nationalbibliografie; detailed bibliographic data are available in the Internet at http://dnb.d-nb.de.
Any brand names and product names mentioned in this book are subject to trademark, brand or patent protection and are trademarks or registered trademarks of their respective holders. The use of brand names, product names, common names, trade names, product descriptions etc. even without a particular marking in this works is in no way to be construed to mean that such names may be regarded as unrestricted in respect of trademark and brand protection legislation and could thus be used by anyone.

Cover image: www.ingimage.com

Publisher: LAP LAMBERT Academic Publishing GmbH & Co. KG
Heinrich-Böcking-Str. 6-8, 66121 Saarbrücken, Germany
Phone +49 681 3720-310, Fax +49 681 3720-3109
Email: info@lap-publishing.com

Printed in the U.S.A.
Printed in the U.K. by (see last page)
ISBN: 978-3-659-18858-9

Dedicated to my Parents

Father-Mr. Ramesh Chandra Thakur

Mother-Smt. Rita Thakur

THE IMPORTANCE OF ENGLISH LANGUAGE FOR PROFESSIONAL AND TECHNICAL EDUCATION

Acknowledgement

I take immense pleasure in presenting this dissertation on this topic, "The Importance of English Language for Professional and Technical Education". This Dissertation is intended to fulfill the requirement for the completion of Post-Graduate in English Language&Literature. So, an attempt has been made to relate the theoretical knowledge imparted in the class-room through lectures and discussion with the practice of professional world.

The real objective behind the preparation of this dissertation is to gain exposure to the actual work environment and including the application, the required knock to guide theoretical knowledge towards facilitating its application. For any professional and technical education, the practical means is to close contact with the prevailing system in an organization, which has a great importance. In this age of liberalization

and globalization of the economic and technological world of English language keeps the vital role in front of professional and technical students.

I wish to express my immense of gratitude to the teachers and students of the professional and technical education.

1

First of all I feel incepted to all those writers whose thoughts and theories have built my concept regarding the subject.

I would like to express my sincere gratitude to my reverent teacher and guide, I would love give my greatest debt is to my Parents, Father, Mr. Ramesh Chandra Thakur and Mother, Mrs. Rita Thakur, my sister, Rashmi and brother Durgesh and all my friends, who give me a precious time for their active help, support and inspiration towards the completion of this dissertation.

Above all, I cordially express my sense of gratitude to almighty, which extended me their unfailing support, affection and encouragement through-out boosted me to complete this work, so easily.

Deepesh Kumar Thakur

Contents   **Page No**

Introduction: -

Chapter-1

English is an International Language and Global Communication, which bridging the gap between modern competitive with the old practices. Therefore, English Language is a medium of technical as well as professional education that how to communicate.

Language is a semiology process that includes symbolic, emotive and indicative functions. It is an expression of the man himself in words in a semiology process and English as a language has multifarious facts or universal features that make it a world language today. Inflexion, relatively fixed words and syntax, the quality of the intonations to express shades of meaning and moods or industriousness are chiefly responsible for its popularity. With a view to reaching out towards the different parts of this world and becoming global, now English language has developed variety of forms, each one correct within its own context, classified as national,regional,social,technical and professional; which is now termed as "ESP",i.e., English for specific purpose. The liberal educational facilities granted to the Indian students, teachers, technocrats and professionals facilitates them to follow both European as well as American English as for as communicative English is concerned. Indian technocrats, business, top executives, bureaucrats, advertiser, teachers, professional and students or the creative writes follow either ascent.

The moderates felt the necessity of making study of English language as optional during the transition period and according to them under the existing circumstances a second knowledge of English is necessary at least for acquiring for higher education. They advocate the importance of learning English language for advancement and growth of world in professional and technical educational empowerment in the country.

It is said by India's first President, Dr. Rajendra Prasad; "English language is an advanced and flexible one and its teaching should not be discarded all together, Indian can't afford to ignore this language."

Indian students have earned a reputation a name in higher education as IT, Space, Science, Technology, Management, Medical and Law where medium of study is in English language. It is thus disputed that learning of English as language is very important as it is not only necessary for higher scientific and managerial research, but it is a linking language which is spoken throughout a large part of this world. It is one of the most popular international language for all diplomatic or political conference, scientific discourse without help of English language as a medium for communication among the members.

English is the medium of answering the questions in almost all the competitive examination like administrative, legal, technical and professional services. Learning of English is very important even in Indian perspective to acquire higher qualification to have pace with the fast progressing world economy, to have communication with world's emissaries, leaders, scientists, professionals, etc.

So, learn from yesterday, live for today, hope for the tomorrow.

It is improving the English speaking capability of students in the field of business and economy, science and technology, agriculture science and entertainment or etc.

English Bridges the gap between modern competitions requirement and ability of technical and professional students.

The development of leadership qualities in the students of each and every area which is communicate as global language. It managed the activity of group goals with English language communication.

5

In the age of globalization and liberalization, English is the only lingua-franca for the entire world. Still, learning of English as a second language poses a number of difficulties for both teachers and learners. How whoever, since then use of language is variegated, it is only when a good command of the language has been achieved .The leaner can proceed with his linguistic adroitness. Teachers and students of English language teaching and researchers in this field will find this book extremely valuable during planning, selection, grading and presentation.

The importance of English language in Indian as a medium of instruction and communication is growing fast since the post-colonial era. The English speaking population in India today exceeds the no of people speaking English in Europe.

How English is Helpful: Global Communication

Today, English has become a link language that helps you converse with people around the world. More so, because the world has become a global village and any one can easily transcend borders for employment. Well, even if you are not looking for employment, there is whole world just waiting for you to explore –trekking, cruise, sightseeing and more. If you have the money and an itch for adventure, then no place is far. English comes in handy when conversing with strangers, getting visa and finding your way around.

But, why people take too much time for fathom this hard fact probably, but only at those initial stages like childhood and adolescence. Latter people are lost and caught in the rigmarole of English courses. They go on to join courses after courses and remain dissatisfied. In the end, lots of money and affords go down the drain. Despite the county wide mushrooming of so called public schools and the children who can't write and read correct English. Why is it confined to the class room only? Why this deteriorating standard in the rural areas when the need to know English the world over is on the rise.

Chapter 2

The evolution of English:

A professional communicative language

English is an Anglo Frisian language or German speaking people from North West germane, Saxons & Angles or Jutland (jutes) evaded what is now known as eastern England around the 5th century AD. It is a matter of debate whether the old English language spread by displacement of the original population, or the native Cents gradually adopted the language and culture of a new ruling class or a combination of both of the process man in Britain.

Whatever their origin these German dialects eventually coalesced to a degree there remain geographical variation and formed what is today called old English. Old English loosely resembles some postal dialects in what is now North West germane and the Netherlands (i.e., Frisian).

Throughout the history of written old English , it retained synthetic structure closer to that of proto land Indo-European , largely adopting west Saxon scribal conventions, While spoken old English becomes increasingly analytic in nature, losing the more complex noun case system , relying more heavily on prepositions and fixed word order to convey meaning . this is evident in the middles English period ,when literature was to and increasing extend recorded with spoken dialectal variation intact after written old English lost its status as a literary language of the nobility . It has been postulated that English retains some traits from a Celtic sub stratum. Later it was influence by the related North Germanic language as Old Norse, spoken by the Vikings who settled namely in the north and east coast down to London, the area non as the Daniela.

The normal conquest of England in 1066 profoundly influenced the evolution of the language. for about 300years after this , the Normans used Anglo-Normal which was close to old French as the language of the court of their low and administration .by the 14th century Anglo normal borrowings had contributed roughly 10,000 words to English , of which 75% remain in use. These include many words pertaining to the legal and administrative fields. It also includes common words for food, such as mutton and beef. The normal influence gave wise to what is now referred to as Middle English .later, during the English Renaissance, many words were borrowed directly from Latin and Greek, leaving a parallel vocabulary that persists into modern times. By the 17th century there was a reaction in some circles against so called inkhorn terms.

During the 15th century , middle English was transformed by the greater vowels shift , the spread of a prestigious south eastern based dialect in the court , administration and academic life or the standardizing effect of printing .early modern English can be traced back to around the Elizabethan period .

Eighteenth century:

Candide, a satire written by Voltaire, took aim at Leibniz as Dr. Pangloss, with the choice of name clearly putting universal language in his sights, but satirizing mainly the optimism of the projector as much as the project. The argument takes the universal language itself no more seriously than the ideas of the speculative scientists and virtuosi of Jonathan Swift's Laputa. For the like-minded of Voltaire's generation, universal language was tarred as fool's gold with the same brush as philology with little intellectual rigour, and universal mythography, as futile and arid directions.

In the 18th century, some rationalist natural philosophers sought to recover a supposed Edenic language. It was assumed that education inevitably took people away from an innate state of goodness they possessed, and therefore there was an attempt to see what language a human child brought up in utter silence would speak. This was assumed to be the Edenic tongue, or at least the lapsarian tongue.

Others attempted to find a common linguistic ancestor to all tongues; there were, therefore, multiple attempts to relate esoteric languages to Hebrew (e.g. Basque, Erse, and Irish), as well as the beginnings of comparative linguistics.

Nineteenth century:

At the end of the 19th century there was a large profusion of constructed languages intended as genuine spoken language. There were created languages which don't belong to any country, and can be learned by everyone. Among these are Solresol, Volapük, and Esperanto, the most spoken constructed language nowadays. At that time, when people dreamed of a better world for everyone, those ideas were readily accepted. With the advent of World Wars and the Cold War these successes were buried.

Twentieth Century:

The constructed language movement[clarification needed] produced such languages as Ido, Latino Sine Flexione, Occidental, and finally the auxiliary language Interlingua.

Twenty First Century:

English remains the dominant language of international business and global communication through the influence of global media and the former British Empire that had established the use of English in regions around the world such as North America, India, Africa, Australia and New Zealand. However, English is not the only language used in global organizations such as in the EU or the UN, because of many countries that do not recognize English as universal language.

Contemporary Ideas:

The early ideas of a universal language with complete conceptual classification by categories are still debated on various levels. Michel Foucault believes such classifications to be subjective, citing Borges' fictional Celestial Emporium of Benevolent Knowledge's Taxonomy as an illustrative example.

A recent philosophical synthesis has also connected Leibniz's interest in environmental engineering with Systems Ecology. It has been proposed that a modern form of Leibniz's Characteristica Universalis is the Energy Systems Language of Systems Ecology, which has been used to develop ecological-economic systems overviews of landscapes, technologies, and Nations. One consequence of this seems to be that Leibniz's Enlightenment project is alive and being applied globally in the evolution of ecological sustainability.

Classification and related languages

English language belongs to the western sub-branch of the Germanic branch of the Indo-European family of languages.

The question as to which is the nearest living relative of English is a matter of discussion. Apart from such English laxities Creole languages such as Tock Psion, Scots spoken primarily in Scotland and parts of Northern Ireland is not a Gaelic language, but is part of the English family of languages: both Scots and modern English are descended from old English, also known as Anglo-Saxon. It is Scots' indefinite status as a language or a dialect of English which complicates definitely calling it is the closest language to English. The closest relatives to English after Scots are the Frisian languages, which are spoken in the Northern Netherland and Northwest Germany. Other less closely related living West Germanic languages include German, low Saxon, Dutch and Africans. The north German languages of Scandinavia are less closely related to English than the West German language.

Many French words are also intelligible to an English speaker, though pronunciations are often quite different; because English absorbed a large vocabulary from Norman and French, via Anglo-Norman after the

Norman Conquest and directly from French in subsequent centuries. As a result , a large portion of English vocabulary is derived from French, with some minor spelling difference, word ending, use of old French spellings,etc.,as well as occasional divergences in meaning, in so-called "Faux-Aims", or false friends.

Geographical Distribution

Over 309 million people speak English as their first language, as of 2005. English today is probably the third largest language by number of native speakers, after Mandarin Chinese and Spanish. However, when combining native and Non-native speakers. It is probably the most commonly spoken language in the third world, though possibly second to a combination of the Chinese language depending on whether or not distinctions in the later are classified as "language" or "Dialects". Estimates that include second language speakers vary greatly from 470 million to over a billion depending on how literacy or mastery is defined. There are some who claim that non-native speakers now outnumber native speakers by a ratio of 3to 1.The countries with the highest populations of native English speakers are, in descending order, United States(215 Million),United Kingdom(58 Million),Canada(17.7 Million),Australia(15 Million),Ireland(3.8 Million),South Africa(3.7 Million) and New Zealand(3.0 to 3.7 Million).

Countries such as Jamaica and Nigeria also have millions of native speakers of dialect continuous ranging from English based Creole to a more standard version of English. Of these nations where English spoken as a second language , India has the largest number of such speakers 'Indian English' and Linguistics professor David Crystal claims that combining native and non-native speakers . India now has more people who speak or understand English than any other country in the world. Following India is the People's Republic of China.

Distribution of Native English speakers by Country   [Crystal 1997]

11

Country	Native Speakers
1. United States	214,809,000
2. United Kingdom	58,200,000
3. Canada	17,694,830
4. Australia	15,013,965
5. Ireland	4,200,000+(approx.)
6. South Africa	3,673,203/21
7. New Zealand	3,500,000+(approx.)
8. Singapore	665,087
9. China	
10. Germany	

English is the primary language in Angola, Antigua, Australia (Australian English), the Bahamas,Barbados,Bermuda,Belize,The British Indian Ocean Territory, the Virgin Islands, Canada(Canadian English),the Cayman Islands,Dominica,the Falkland Islands,Gibraltar,Grendansey(Guernsey English),Guyana, Ireland (Hibernian English) ,Isle of Man (Manx English), Jamaica (Jamaican English), Jersey, Montserrat,Nauru,New Zealand (New Zealand English),Pitcairn Islands, Saint Helena, Saint Lucia, Saint Kitts &Nevis, Saint Vicent & The Grenadines,Singapore,South Georgia, South Sandwich Islands, Trinidad and Tobago, The Turks and Ciaos Islands, The United Kingdom, The U.S. Virgin Islands, The United States (Various forms of American English).

In many other countries, where English is not the most spoken language, it is an official language, these countries include Bostwana,Cameroon,Fiji, The Federated States of Micronesia, Ghana, Gambia,India,Kiribati,Lesotho,Liberia,Kenya,Madagascar,Malta, The Marshall Islands,Namibia,Nigeria,Pakistan,Papua New Guinea, The Philippines, Puerto Rico,Rwanda,The Solomon Islands,Samoa,Seychelles, Sierra Leon,Sri Lanka,Swaziland,Tanzania,Uganda,Zambia, Zimbabwe etc......It is also one of the 11 official languages that are given equal status in South Africa (South African English). English is also an important language in several former colonies or current dependent territories of the United Kingdom and the United States such as in Hong Kong and Mauritius.

English is not an official language either in the United States or the United Kingdom. Although the United States federal government has no official languages, English has been given official status by 30 of the state governments.

English in India

Information on Language:

Languages in India officially English has a status of assistant language, but in fact it is the most important language in India. After Hindi it is the most commonly spoken language in India and probably the most read and written language in India. Indians who know English will always try to show that they know English. English symbolizes in Indians minds, better education, better culture and higher intellect. Indians who know English often mingle it with Indian languages in their conversations. It is also usual among Indians to abruptly move to speak fluent in the middle of their conversations. English also serves as the communicator among Indians who speak different language. English is very important in some systems- legal, financial, educational, business in India.Untill the beginning of 1990's foreign movies in India weren't translated or dubbed in Indian languages, but were broadcast in English and were meant for English speakers only. The reason Indians give such importance English is related to the fact that India was a British colony.

When the British started ruling India, they searched for Indian mediators who could help them to administer India. The British turned to high caste Indians to work for them. Many high caste Indians, especially the Brahmans worked for them. The British policy was to create an Indian class who should think like the British or as it was said then in Britain, Indian in blood and colour but English in taste, in opinions and morals and intellect. The British also established in India universities based on British models with emphasis on English. These Indians also got their education in British universities. The English Christian missionaries came to India from 1813 and they also built schools at primary level for the Indians in which the language of instruction was local language. Later on missionaries built high schools with English as the language of instruction which obliged the Indians who wanted to study to have a good knowledge of English. The British rulers began building their universities in India from 1857. English became the first language in Indian education. The modern leaders of that era in India also supported English language and claimed it to be the main key towards success. Indian who knew good English were seen as the new elite of India. Many new schools were established in which the language of instruction was English. According to the British laws the language of instruction at university level was English and therefore schools that emphasized English were proffered by ambitious Indians. Even after India's independence, English remained the main language of India. Officially it was given a status of an assistant language and was supposed to terminate officially after 15 years of India's independence, but it still remains the important language of India.

Even today schools in India that emphasis English are considered better schools and the same is the case at university levels, even though there is a trend towards Indiannisation. In the 1970s and 1980s about one third of the Indian schools had English language. For most of these students, English is their first language and it is easier for them to communicate, read and write in English than in Indian languages including their mother tongues.

Just like the American, Australians or even the British who have their unique English words and phrases, the Indians also have their own unique English. The Indians and the Indian English language press uses many words derived from Indian languages, especially from Hindi. Other than that, the Indian ascent is sometimes difficult for non-Indians to understand. There are some Indian pronunciations that don't exist in non Indian languages. The British also had problems with that and they caused some changes in Indian words, so, that they could pronounce them. Even the Indians started using these changed words and made them part of their English.

Two examples of such changed are Curry and Sari.....

According to Kachru, there have been three phrases in the introduction of bilingualism in English in India. The first one of them, the Missionary phase, was initiated around 1614 by Christian missionaries. The second phase, the demand from the South Asian public in the eighteenth century was considered to come about through local demand, as some scholars were of the opinion that the spread of English was the result of the demand and willingness of local people to learn the language. There were prominent spokesmen for English. Kachru mentions two of them, Raja Ram Mohan Roy (1772-1833) and Rajunath Hari Navalkar (fl.1770). Roy and Navalkar, among others were persuading the officials of the East India Company to give instruction in English, rather than in Sanskrit or Arabic. They thought that English would open the way for people to find out about scientific developments of the west knowledge of

15

Sanskrit, Persian and Arabic or of Indian vernaculars would not contribute to this goal.

A letter of Raja Ram Mohan Roy address to Lord Amherst (1773-1857) from the year 1823 is often presented as evidence of local demand for English. Roy embraced European learning, and in his opinion, English provided Indians with the key to all knowledge, all the really useful knowledge which the world contains. In the letter, Roy expresses his opinion that the available funds should be used for employing European gentlemen of talent and education to instruct the natives of India in Mathematics, Natural Science, Philosophy, Chemistry, Anatomy and other useful Sciences, which the natives of Europe have carried to a degree of perfection that has raised them above the inhabitants of other parts of the world. Roy's letter has been claimed to be responsible for starting the Oriental_Anglicist controversy, the controversy over which educational policy would be suitable for India. The third phase, the government policy begun in 1765, when the East India Company's authority was stabilized. English was established firmly as the medium of instruction and administration. English language became popular, because it opened paths to employment and influence. English of the subject Indians became gradually a widespread means of communication.

During the governor generalship Lord William Bentinck in early nineteenth century, India saw many reforms. English became the language of record the government and higher courts and government support was given to the cultivation of Western learning and science through the medium of English.

English in Independent India

English was established firmly as the medium of instruction and administration by the British Raj (1765-1947).Indian education was ever greater anglicized as English language became rooted in an alien linguistic, cultural, administrative and educational setting. It becomes the language of the Elite, press and Administration. The first universities were established in India on 1857 at Bombay, Calcutta and Madras. English became accepted as the language of elite and of Pan Indian Press. English Newspaper, Magazines, Reports, Notices had an influential reading public.

India after becoming Independent in 1947 was left with a colonial language. In this case English as the language of government. It was thought that the end of the British Raj would mean the slow but sure demise of English language in South Asia. This, of course has not happened. The penetration of English in these societies is greater that it has ever been.

Nationalist imperative wanted that English continue to be used. Nationalist motivations were of the opinion that an indigenous Indian language should be adopted as the official language. Hindi seemed most qualified for that, since it had more native speakers than any other Indian language and was already widely used in interethnic communication.

In addition, it was thought that linguistic unity was a prerequisite for political and national unity. Thus, Hindi was designated by the constitution as the language of communication between and within the states. It was to replace English within 15 years; the plan was that Hindi would be promoted so that it might express all parts of the "Composite culture of India". There were several problems with selecting Hindi, since the protests were often violent e.g., the riots in Tamilnadu in May 1963, protesting against the imposition of Hindi, the government wanted to adapt a policy which would help to maintain the status quo. First of all, Hindi is not evenly distributed throughout the country; e.g., in Tamilnadu, in the south only 0.0002 percent of the people claimed knowledge of Hindi or Urdu. Secondly, it was thought that the speakers of other languages would be offended by its selection, other Indian languages. For example Tamil and Bengali had as much right to be national languages as Hindi. The other Indian communities felt they would be professionally, politically and socially disadvantaged were Hindi given the central role. Thirdly, Hindi was thought to need vocabulary development before it could be used efficiently as a language of government. In spite of these problems, Hindi was chosen as the national language in the constitution and English was to be replaced by Hindi in fifteen years' time. However, due to the continuous opposition in the south, this replacement was not politically possible. In 1967 a law passed which allowed the use of both Hindi and English for all official purposes or that situation still exists.

The controversy between Hindi, Urdu and Hindustani made the case for Hindi even worse. Support for Hindustani almost ended with Independence, Hindi's supporter's enthusiasm was not also channeled in a constructive direction. As a result, English continues to be a language of both power and prestige.

In India, English has gradually acquired socially and administratively the most dominant roles. The power and prestige of language was defined by the domains of language use. Ultimately the legal system, the national media and important professions were conducted in English. The skilled professional Indian became the symbol of westernization and modernization. Raja Ram Mohan Roy was committed to the idea that the "European gentlemen of talent and education" should be appointed to instruct the natives of India. English came too used by Indians, as well.

By 1920s English had become the language of political discourse, intra-national administration and law. A language associated with liberal thinking. Even after the colonial period ended, English maintained its power over local languages.

English was eventually used against Englishmen, their roles and an intention as it became the language of resurgence of nationalism and political awakening, medium, ironically was the alien language. Mohan Das Karamchand Gandhi (1869-1948), for instance although struggled to create consensus for an acceptable native variety as the national language which expressed in his message to the elite in English.

Official language generally used for government administration, law, media, and as one of the languages of education, at least secondary and higher education on a nationwide basis.

Positive and Negative aspects of the Dominance of English

In an ideal world, everybody would have linguistic access to everything. If access is denied or hindered in some way, however, a power differential, whether accidental or intended is engendered. English clearly dominates in the world today and because English is the acknowledge lingua-franca of science, technology and business, the field of English for specific purposes-ESP, holds a pivotal position in regard to the use or abuse of this linguistic power. It is therefore important for the ESP profession to articulate the positive and negative aspects of the current dominance of English.

For example in being the universal language of air and sea traffic control. It believed that true linguistic emancipations would be achieved when everyone in a speech.

English is Medium

Every Indian University teaches in English and most Indian Universities consider a good knowledge of English as a pre-requisite to pursuing academic studies. For foreign students weak in language, most of the colleges and Universities conduct special English communication courses. The attitude of teachers and parents helps in generating interest among students. In our region, teachers put up very little effort and English is considered as a burden. The parents, on the other hand, feel that English being a foreign language may take their children away from their culture. Thus, nobody inculcate the reading habit among children. Buy English story books are unheard of as it means waste of money. Teachers tell students that English is a foreign language, and make them feel that it is a burden. Later, students grow up with this idea, which will benefit for the students. Grammar was never taught in our school because the teacher was busy giving tuitions. I could never learn its correct usage and thus suffered in my profession. The teachers in rural areas do not explain the pronunciation and meaning of difficult words. So, one does not develop interest in subject. A student of creative writing said that, I too am a product of a rural school, but one of my juniors from a public school was amazed at my written as well as spoken English. The reason was that our teachers used to take active interest in students' progress. They would write on the blackboard and explain every difficult word so as to make the subject interesting. Thus, the students could enjoy reading, writing and speaking. Today, the fault lays both at the teachers' and students level. While the teachers have commercialized education and are less interested in students' welfare the students too don't inculcate the reading habit among themselves.

The importance of English has declined and there is more emphasis on indigenous languages. There has been a tremendous gap between colonialism and the contemporary society. So, the domination of English and its hold over society has diminished. The focus has shifted from grammatically right language to tech-savvy. For example, if you are doing a project, you can use English language software where you need not depend on grammar. You have to know the know-how, now employment opportunities do not depended upon English alone. New subjects like functional English communication skills etc. are being introduced in colleges. Orientation is changing in this computer world.

But one should know good English to aspire high and probably in rural areas, the people are not aware of the fact. To learn the language, one needs to have a social set up convincing the learner why it is important to learn good English. The idea of English as a superior language is declining, but you nevertheless need it. Thus it feels that learning English is a must these days.

Importance of English Now a Days

English is becoming more and more important today. That is why before starting teaching people must tell them about it. It is not only in words, but also in practice. Teaching English is easy that it is rather difficult to explain such students how important it is to know English now days. In a survey a lot of people who learn English but they don't seem to know it until they realize its importance.

Just a few centuries ago, English was spoken by just five to seven million people on one. Relatively Small Island and the language consisted of dialects spoken by monolinguals. Today there are more non native than native users of English, it become the linguistic key used for opening borders. It is a global medium with local identities and messages. English has become a world language, spoken by at least 750 million people. It is more widely spoken and written than any other language, even Latin has ever been. It can indeed be said to be the first truly global language. English is now a days the dominant or official language in over 60 countries.

The increase in use of English in Asia as "overwhelming". At present the estimated population using English in Asia adds up to 350 million. India is the third largest English using population in the world, after USA and UK. Literatures in English are now a day's recognized as part of the national literatures and English is also recognized in the overall language policy of the nation. The language has penetrated deeply in the society, which has in its turn resulted in several varieties of English in India. The development of those new varieties is connected with historical and social factors. The new English's have all their own contexts of function and usage and they also in their turn affected the native varieties of English. Indian English is used mainly by Indians whose native language is local or regional dialects. It is a minority language, but yet a language of national affairs and its status is often called into question. Bailey puts it not only by foreigners with their ideas of proper English but also by Indians who remain ambivalent about its distinctive features and uncertain about its future. In fact many of transplanted kinds of English are so attuned to the idea of a foreign standard of propriety that their independence remains partial. The out emergence of these new varieties has raised questions concerning the power of English language, questions of identity and new pragmatics of the language in new, foreign surroundings. The spread of English across different cultures and languages has meant the diversification of English, which in turn raises questions about the standardization of English.

The purpose of this study will be to study language attitudes in India, especially attitudes towards English and to analyze the use of languages in different domains family, friendship, neighborhood, transactions, education, government, employment, additionally the aim is also to find out about the informants preference for the model of the variety of English in India.

Dialects and Regional varieties

The expansion of the British Empire and since World War –II, the practices of the United States have spread English throughout the globe. Because of that global spread, English has developed a host of English dialects and English based Creole languages and pidgins.

The major verities' of English including most cases with several sub-varieties such as Cockney slang within British English. Newfoundland English within Canadian English and African-American vernacular English, 'Ebonics' and Southern American English. English is a pluricentric language without a central language authority like France's Academic franchise and although no variety is clearly considered the only standard, there are a number of ascents considered to be more prestigious, such as Received Pronunciation in Britain.

Scots developed largely independently from the same origins, but following the Acts Union 1707 a process of language attrition began, where by successive generations adopted more and more features from

English causing dialectalisation. Whether it is now a separate language or a dialect of English is better described as Scottish English is in dispute. The pronunciation, grammar and lexis of the traditional forms differ, sometimes substantially from other varieties of English. Because of the wide use of English as a second language, English speakers have many different ascents, which often signal the speakers' native dialect or language. For the more distinctive characteristics of regional ascents, see Regional accent of speakers, and for the more distinctive characteristics of regional dialects

Just an English it has borrowed words from many different languages over history ; English loanwords now appear in a great many languages around the world , indicative of technological and cultural influence of its speakers. Several pidgins and Creole languages have formed using an English base, such as Jamaican Creole, Nigerian pidgin, and Tok Pisin. There are many words in English coined to describe forms of particular non-English languages that contain a very high proportion of English words. Franglais, for example, is used to describe French with very high English word content; it is found on the Channel Islands. Another variant, spoken in the border bilingual region of Quebec in Canada, is called Frankish.

Constructed varieties of English

Basic English is simplified for easy international use. It is used by manufactures and other international businesses to write manuals and communicate. Some English schools in Asia teach it as a practical subset of English for use by beginners.

Special English is a simplified version of English used by the Voice of America. It uses a vocabulary of only 1500 words.

English reform is an attempt to improve collectively upon the English language. Sea speak, Air speak and Police speak, all based on restricted vocabularies, were designed by Edward Johnson in the 1980s to aid international cooperation and communication in specific areas. There is also a tunnel speak for use in the channel Tunnel. English as a Lingua-Franca for Europe and Euro-English are concepts of standing English for use as a second language in continental Europe. Manually coded English, a variety of systems have been developed to represent the English language with hand signals, designed primarily for use in deaf education. These should not be confused with true sign languages such as British sign language and American Sign Language used Anglophone countries, which are independent and not based on English.

Euro-English terms are English translations of European concepts that are not native to English speaking countries. Because of United Kingdom's and even the Republic of Ireland's involved in the European Union, the usage focuses on non British concepts. This kind of Euro-English was parodied when English was made one of the constituent languages of European. English is spoken by nearly five million people throughout the world. It is the official language of nearly fifty nations, which is the mother tongue of the sixty million people of small British Island spread all over world for historical, political and social reasons known to most of us. The explorers, colonizers and empire builders, Bruisers made a gift of their language including several other things to the world.

The first decade of this century witness an amazing spread, expansion with happy acceptance of this language as it happens to first language of several countries that are called the countries of first world such as the United States , Canada, Australia, New Zealand and a number of Pacific Islands. The official status of English in several International bodies and it we as auxiliary language in the world establish it as an International language. Language is not a national phenomenon in the sense that it is created by humans. The individuals need to express their fulfilled through language and society is in a way structured through it. Language helps an individual's shape his or herself. It is a medium of expression but the complex nature of human languages contrast with the animal languages makes it an institute in itself. Animal languages for example, the language of bees is instinctive and it allows little space for an individual bee to differ from other bees completely through language. It does not only help

24

an individual to communicate others but also to express his or her distinctive features of personality through it or perhaps shape or make those features.

Our world today heavily depends on the technological and professional advancements and the rapid changes in these advancements world outsmart all predictions about the nature of life in times to come. The students of technical and professional colleges besides being educated in the conventional pedagogical sense need to be trend to live skillfully. Education imparted to the future generation should be such as to enable them to live naturally and accommodate themselves efficiently with the changing patterns of life. The role of English language is a unifying one. Several nations' use it is as a link language and all kinds of books are being written English language and if not written one translated into this language all over world. The cultural impact of this language in our country in particular is immense. The educated people almost all over the world speak this language. The main purpose of technical and professional colleges is to equip the students with sufficient amount of skill so that they are able to survive in this fast changing world.

The explosion of knowledge that is taking place in the world these days can be accessed only through a familiarity with English language. It seems that English is key to the storehouse of knowledge. The observation made by Kothari commission that English would play a vital role in higher education as an important library language had grains of truth in it. In order to discuss and assess the relevance of English language with reference to the technical and professional colleges in India we need to keep in mind the multilingual culture of our country. In order to follow lectures and to be able to use the available study material to the student of technical colleges need to be good as English language. Not only the perception, interpretation and understanding of the world depend on a mastery over a language but also the expression of the individual as well as simply depend upon this.

The learners of a language keep a few basic things in mind. The human language has more than one representation. The existence of it in our mind and in the written and spoken form results into three kinds of its representation. The language in written form is orthographic representation and third is psychological form. In Hindi it is claimed that the orthographic representation correspondents to the phonetic representation but it is not the whole truth. The real purpose of education is to transfer the knowledge to the masses, and purpose of academics is to transfer it perfectly. Even after over forty of independence English occupies an important place in every walk of life. Whether it is social, educational, administrative, scientific, industrial or commercial life in the country, we find English taking the place of honour.

Standard Language

When we described the sounds, words and sentences of English we were in fact concentrating on the features of only one variety, usually labeled Standard English. This is the variety which forms the basis of printed English in newspapers and books, which is used in mass media and which is taught in schools. It is the variety we normally try to teach those who want to learn English as a second language. It is clearly associated with education and broadcasting in public contexts and is more easily described in terms of written language, i.e., vocabulary, spelling, grammar than the spoken language.

A to Z: -- Teaching a competency which makes teaching-learning effective in professional and technical education.

A – Alertness

B- Business like attitude to keep busy worthwhile task.

C- Clarity and co-operation teaching-learning.

D- Devotion and discovery.

E- Enthusiasm, expecting students to learn and evaluated them.

F- Feedback for the guidance of the learner and the teacher.

G- Goal setting and achieving them.

H- Hard-work, honest work, humility and honour.

I- Involvement of students.

J- Judicious attitude and just action.

K- Knowledge of the student, subject matter and oneself.

L- Liking, learning with daily experiences of life activities.

M- Morality and motivation.

N- Need based learning

O- Objective and providing out of class room learning experiences.

P- Patience and praising students who needed.

Q- Quiz organizing for monitoring & learning process.

R- Relationships and review of data.

S- Stimulation of situational factor.

T- Tolerance and the technology of the teaching-learning.

U- Unbiased attitude and unexpected.

V- Variety of learning experiences.

W- Warmth and wisdom willing.

X- X-ray of the learning process.

Y- Yearning.

Z- Zeal with knowledge.

Language is an organization of sounds of vocal symbols, the sounds produced from the mouth with the help of various organs of speech to convey some meaningful message. It also means that speech is primary to writing and reading the language speech and tone. There are several languages in the world which have no writings systems, yet they are language because they are spoken. Music and singing also employ vocal sounds, but they are not language. Language is the most powerful, convenient and permanent means and form of communication. This is the set of conventional communicative signals used by humans for communication in a community. Language is this sense is a possession of a social group, comprising and indispensable set of rules which permits its members to relate to each other, to interact with each other, to co-operate with each other. It is a social institution which can so it exists in society, it means of nourishing and developing culture and establishing human relations. It is a member of society that a human being acquires a language. Now-a- days 3450 languages are facing extinction worldwide. Communication is the key speech is part of our cultural identity.

Effective Communication in English

The English language contains about 490,000 words plus about 300,000 technical words. It is doubtful if any individual uses more than 60,000 words. Written English uses about 10,000 words while spoken English, by the better educated, uses about 5,000 words.

Effective communication in the English language requires that we follow a few simple rules that can be learnt and practiced by anyone. We just need to keep in mind the purpose of communication.

The purpose of communication
- Issue, receive, interpret, act on commands
- Maintain relations - personal and business
- Structure the environment – share information, defines jobs.

This can easily and more effectively be achieved by being:
'Direct, Simple, Brief, Vigorous and Lucid' and the way to do this is to:

- Prefer the familiar word to the far-fetched;
- Prefer the single word to the circumlocution;
- Prefer the short word to the long;
- Prefer the Saxon word to the Romance;

- Prefer the concrete word to the abstract.

Prefer the familiar word to the far-fetched:

If you can use	Do not use
Buy	purchase or acquire
measure	quantify

Prefer the short word to the long

If you can use	Do not use
Hope	expectations
Kind	categories

Prefer the single word to the circumlocution

If you can use	Do not use
Act	take action on the issue
Often	in several instances

Prefer the Saxon word to the Romance

Saxon	Romance
earnings	profit
Fall	depreciate

Prefer the concrete word to the abstract:

If you can use	Do not use
lorries, cars	transportation facilities
Door	Entrance

EFFECTIVE COMMUNICATION IN ENGLISH

1. *Clarify ideas before communicating*: Systematically think through the message and consider who will be receiving it and/or affected by it.

2. *Examine the true purpose of communication*: One must ask himself/herself this question – what am I really aiming to accomplish with this message? The use of language can then be suitably adjusted.

3. *Take the entire environment, physical and human, into consideration*: Questions such as, what is being said, to whom and when are very important. Your skill lies in how you say it and, of course, your timing. Adapt your language to the environment.

4. *Be careful of the overtones and the basic content of the message*: The listener will be affected by they way you put across your message. Your tone and facial expressions are also to be considered.

5. *Use crisp language and be clear*: It is very important that the words are well chosen and that you stay as crisp and concise as possible. In other words use minimum words to send across the message and convey useful information.

6. *Follow-up on communication*: One must solicit feedback in ensuring that the receiver has understood the message. If the person has not understood, tone down the language.

7. *Be a good listener*: By concentrating on the receiver's response you can ensure his extent of interest in you and also if he is concentrating.

Avoid:

* Use of long words
* Using new words
* Jargon

* Assuming they know
* Preconceptions, prejudices
* Information overload
* Noise
* Information filtering
* Lack of trust

Chapter-3

Importance of English language studies in Science & Management education

Technical field and language are both intricately intertwined and bring forth the latent personality in ourselves. The pre-requisites of presentation of our nation talents and technical skills are good communication skills and proper interaction. Presentation of national skills at an international conference demands the foundation to be very strong in English. The most interesting and felicitating aspect of English is that all technical and professional institutions have made it a compulsory subject as in syllabus of technical or professional universities.

The role of English is quite indispensable for its required interaction between institutions and teaching staff or students and among students themselves. English is a language that is accepted in latter day world in recognizing every process in technical fields. Speak of Astrophysics or Nuclear Physics or any kind of formats, formulations, communications as well as documentations are made in English.

Human beings are better recognized than other creatures for their effective medium of communication. We are to realize the importance of communication skills if we want to manifest our potentialities. How can we people expect our exhibition and recognition of technological products in the arena of global trade and commerce effectively without proper presentation skills? Well let me say these are the very essence of business aspect in technical field. Speaking in particular communication and ability in highlighted by one's gestures & postures that we call "Body Language", this shows the mindset of one's idea. For instance, our eye expressions, hand movements and smiles while conversing with someone, especially with an interviewer or board Member. There has to be an absolute wide awareness amongst students for building up an impressive body language. New inexperienced but potential and innovative technocrats wouldn't be able to convince the executive board members unless he or she has dynamic ambidextrous interpersonal skills. Language on pen or paper has to be put forth in words be captivating as well as grammatically correct. Well, I am speaking in proper accent and phonetics. We, Indians generally are backward in internationally acclaimed pronunciations. There should be a mass launch of accent improvement classes and seminars in all technical institutions. There are some facets of personality development, which are sure to inculcate our strengths inherent in us manifold. I accentuate that communication and presentation skills as well as personality and body language access, should be stress to definite degrees in our institutions if we are to project forward with dogged confidence and optimism. I am absolutely sorry to say that all and sundry are not showing much inclination towards the procurement of efficiency in this medium of communication, because awareness is still lacking in us. And until and unless everyone is equally contributing towards the enhancement of a common medium. The inability to understand and use English well can make many routine activities such as reading in a bus schedule or help wanted advertisements. While situations like these can be frustrating, many people who have limited English proficiency face far more serious consequences when trying to manage their own health.

In today's changing global environment many organizations have voiced the need for new graduates of engineering programmes to have a stronger soft skills emphasis. For example, employers need new graduates to be good communicators and to work in multidisciplinary team of diverse cultural background and different personality styles. Therefore, learning institutions that are able to align with industry demands to produce graduating engineers and managers with the right kind of skills will reap substantial benefits. The integration of project management skills into the University engineering, medical, management curriculum offers one solution for training and preparing students with the necessary transferable hard and soft skills from the classroom workplace. Unfortunately, essential non-technical skills are still lacking among engineering & management graduates because of most engineering and management schools provide students with little practical experience and few applications competencies. These are the key features where the emphasis should be laid on:

➢ Improving communication and links between industry employers and educationists to create a clearer direction for student learning.

➢ Making the curriculum content more relevant to current and future needs of engineering organizations.

➢ Restructuring/Redefining classroom pedagogy, so that it incorporates essential skill attributes.

➢ Encouraging students to obtain the needed skill attributes through a structured and well planned industrial internship programme, class projects/thesis involvement with student and professional organizations and campus organizations.

➢ Standardizing and making essential soft skills education compulsory in the engineering curriculum.

Changes in the engineering curriculum over the last decade have not been dynamic enough to keep pace with a rapidly changing marketplace. Consequently, many graduates lack the essential skills on which to build new learning experiences. Thus curriculum changes are needed for engineering schools to stay relevant. Undoubtedly, this issue will present a big challenge for educators to design and implement effective learning strategies for soft skills education into the engineering curriculum. A stronger emphasis on acquiring and practicing soft skills, while at University is likely to better prepare students for the workplace. Not all students possess Project Management skills at attributes naturally and hence students need help in acquiring soft skills techniques to handle human relationship issues that match employer expectations. Other ways of encouraging soft skill development include co-education, internships, mentoring and by engaging students in practical real world design problems and case studies. It should provide students with valuable opportunities for teamwork, problem solving, planning, scheduling, people management and communications.

Language study has special significance in technical and professional education. Expressing in technical or professional field, one should avoid vagueness and unnecessary elaboration. So, we can conclude that expression in this field should have precision and clarity. To be successful in this respect a student should possess adequate selective vocabulary and should learn how to utilize this vocabulary to serve his purpose. The language learning process of technical and professional students should have a definite orientation. Besides a command over general vocabulary, he should be proficient in the vocabulary relevant to his subject and work. These are the primary equipments that can add with sound imagination, intelligence and clarity of thought. These equipments will shape a satisfactory communicative skill. In the field of science and technology, clarity of expression is very significant. Here ideas should not be expressed in ambiguous and complex terms as is done in philosophy and at time in literature. Such tendencies will the process of communication in the field of technical and professional. So the basic necessity is to create an orientation in the mind of such students. Besides comprehension work and the paragraph writing, some model writing should be presented to the students who will serve as silent teachers. Thus it becomes clear that effective and practical classroom teaching and individual endeavor are equally important in the process of language learning.

Role of Engineers:

Now, let us see the evolution of roles in career for engineers. Who join in industries as technical hands gradually with the passage of time, they become mangers as their responsibilities increase in the managerial field. Finally, an engineer is required to perform as a leader, so in this process of transformation, a technocrat is required to work with people, understand and develop interpersonal skills, build relationship and network with people in various hierarchical positions, social stature and intellectual levels. Engineers also need to command and motivate a team of people having diverse background and qualifications. Needless to say here that whatever be one's technical skills, without a command over communication and human skills, success is likely to remain an unachieved dream in life. To discuss the stages of learning this is absolutely essential in the spoken field for a technocrat. In the field of technology method of learning, method of self study and the benefit of learning are necessary. These stages are shown in process given below:-

General conversation—Formal&Informal=Telephonic

Answering Interview---frequently asked questions.

Public speaking ---Seminar, Meeting, Anchoring=Discussion.

In the method of listening pronunciation, intonation and vocabulary are needed. Pronunciation deals with proper accented or dissented. It is clearly intimate our emotion with proper emphasis and our narration should be clear. In the same way we should absorb strong vocabularies, phonetic device and thorough knowledge for reading. Our voice should be clear and bold with good pronunciation or intonation. In the field of self study reading English Journal and books, listening to news on radio or television or group discussion supports a lot for improvement. Taking structure into account grammatical correctness is above all important in the field of communication.

In learning English there are different areas where telephone, debate, interviews taking initiative in conversation with proper manner. It differ with speaking informal situation, introducing a person to another person, a discussion in formal situation on a specific topic, speaking to a celebrity, simple conversation in day to day life, a business talk delivering lecture and so on. The problem areas we face in communication mostly are on breathing, understanding, pausing, clarity, voice shyness, pronunciation, vocabularly, structure, grammar accuracy, listening etc. It varies men to men like different types of speakers, is, which they are slow talkers, nasal talkers, shirkers, lazy lips, foghorn, husky and so on. At times speech blemishes occur and these blemishes are apologetic beginning, jargon, meaningless words and phrases, copycat, lack of audience contact, repetition, and lack of grace, enthusiasm and "er" habits.

To explain more elaborately, the learning areas in the communication are the ability to ask question, pronunciation, general fluency, structural accuracy, communicate effectively, proper vocabulary skill, ability to answer with appropriate vocabulary and structure. So it is need for rectify our spoken English, It helps to need and enjoy public gathering, meeting and party. Any one always concentrates on their own business by fluency of communication. We must have perfect endurance to survive in an English speaking environment with self-respect. In order to upgrade our speaking skills it is a continuous process of improvement without any full stop. We should get practice in meeting, speaking different languages, recording, discussing, reading magazines or journals, listening to radio, watching television and learning new words. Good language teaching is teaching with or without technology or science also shown the methodology which you use. Regardless of video formats like analog, digital and student made pre-packaged on the web etc., teachers still need to evaluate their video technology in terms of language goals. Whether a teacher is just starting out with technology or whether he/she is known around the school as a techno-gadget queen, the evaluation process it's same.

There are four phases of evaluating and implementing video technology:

Content and Instructional Presentation

In the first phase, teachers evaluate the video technology for its content and instructional presentation. This means how it fit with the outlined goals and objectives of the lesson or the course. Goals should always be tied to student's achievement and progress. For example, "to infuse video into my lessons" is not a good goal. While you may be able to reflect an increase over the previous years of percentage of videos you showed, the goal is not tied with students achieving mastery of the content or language. The goal should be linked to a year end assessment or other standards based means of determine, if students have reached an established level of performance. To establish the goal, write it in simple, direct language that can be understood by almost any audience. An example of a good goal would be "to improve students" persuasive oral presentations. This goal is accurate, complete and non-trival, first ask,"How can I accomplish this goal"; then ask "can I use technology to realize this goal"?

Planning for Instruction

The second phase of evaluating and implementing video technology is planning for instruction for listing the students, who need to accomplish the goal. Using the persuasive oral presentation example, you would list the skilled students would need to accomplish this task. Be precise with example if any want to good oral presentations, they might want the students to have good eye contact, appropriate gestures and a strong persuasive introduction with facts to support it.

Designing Task for Students

In phase three, the instructor needs to design tasks for the student to practice the skills taught. As you design task, include the instructional strategies for teaching the skill. In the persuasive oral thematic presentation example, you might teach the students the skills of (1) Organizing around a topic sentence using a Mini-lesson in lecture format and (2) Including supporting details using direct, whole class instruction as your instructional strategy. Imagine your thematic unit is 'animals'. You teach the students to make a controversial topic sentence such as "Dogs make better pets than cats".

The class might brainstorm three supporting details:

(a)   Dogs come when you call

(b)   Dogs will go swimming with you

(c)   Dogs are more companionable than cats.

Using peer-mediated learning as your instructional strategy, you ask the students to practice their speeches. They make introductory and concluding remarks.

Assessment

In phase four, the instructor needs to assess whether or not the goal was met. Did the students accomplish the task during the guided practice activity, can they now do it on their own, how do you know, how do the students know if they have mastered the skills? The teacher should provide a rubric or scoring guide, which the students can make based on the prepared video models they analyzed. Students should be able to fill in the scoring guide during guided practice. These should be aligned to the skills and standards expected by your programme, school, district or state. For the persuasive oral presentation, you might want to make sure students include a strong, controversial topic sentence with three convincing details and supporting evidence. You might want students to pause after each thought, make eye contact with everyone in the room, have good posture and use correct grammar or pronunciation.

In the oral presentation example, it is possible to use all the latest in video gadgetry. The movies examples can be shown on DVD and students can use the special features to analyze the persuasive language and idiomatic expressions of the characters in many languages including their first language if it's available. Students can use the latest digital video cameras to make their own speeches and put them on the web. They use all the language skills speaking, listening, reading and writing to accomplish this task. They do the things that know help students learn language, negotiating meaning with their peers, viewing models, practicing the target language, using the first language, participating in hands on activities, incorporating all learning styles and modalities and having clear expectations through a rubric or scoring guide.

One newcomer to English language education with research beginning in the 1960's is English for specific purposes ESP, a discipline that has experienced remarkable growth in the last 20 years in numbers of specialists, programs and publications as well as in quality of research education. ESP is English language instruction designed to meet the specific learning needs of learner or a group of learners within a specific time frame for which instruction in general English will not suffice. Most often, this instruction involves orientation to specific spoken and written English, usually unfamiliar to the average speaker, which is required to carry out specific academic or workplace tasks.

Chapter-4

Impact of English Language for the development in Professional and Technical students:

Communication of Professional & Technocrats

It is stated that employers now seek technical and professional graduates and post graduates with skills in English language:-

➤ Awareness of the social implications their disciplines.

➤ Managerial and Technical skills.

➤ Understanding of other points of view and other culture.

➤ Confidents and competence to work in international environment.

The professional profile of a modern qualified engineer should include well-developed communication skills and high English language proficiency to help him achieve success in the modern highly competitive global work arena. In the process of educating future engineers special emphasis on English for science and Technology (EST) becomes necessary. Students of engineering and Technology are the main stakeholders of EST.

English in India is no more the language of the alien rulers. It has been accepted as an Indian language by the Sahitya Academy since 1960. In a multilingual country like India, English serves as Lingua-Franca. People of different regional language can exchange their thoughts and ideas through English and benefit by it. In this respect, communicative English plays a very important role in India. Now a lot of books are being translated from various regional languages into English. The exchange or thoughts through English will definitely help broaden the horizon of literature as a whole. But unless English that is used in translation is communicative, the objective of translation will be defeated. On the whole, the art of writing or speaking should be like a window of plain glass through which the writer's or speaker's meaning becomes clearly visible.

In order to identify their English language needs, the researcher designed and administered a questionnaire.

Objectives of the Study

➢　To find out the language needs of the engineering students the authors teach.

➢　To test their basic understanding of the nature of EST.

➢　To discover their expectations regarding their teachers of English.

➢　To identify a specific set of competencies for teachers of English at engineering colleges.

The communication is a dynamic human activity and must keep pace with people's life style with their business and other occupation. There are inevitable changes in English language style as technology influences all that we do.

Understand your analysis.

Understand your colleagues, seniors, peers, and subordinators.

Understand the message purpose and content.

Understand the organizational structure and policies.

Keep an open mind.

Develop the art of listening.

Learn to be a good listener.

Overcome the sources of knowledge.

English as a Global Language: A world communication

Since English is so widely spoken, it has often been referred to as a global language, the lingua-franca of the modern era. While English is not an official language in most countries, it is currently the language most often taught as a second language around the world. Some linguists believe that it is no longer the exclusive cultural sign of native English speakers, but is rather a language that is absorbing aspects of cultures worldwide as it continues to grow. It is by international treat, the official language for aerial and maritime communications as well as one of the official languages of the European Union, the United Nations and most international athletic organizations including the International Olympic Committee.

English is the language most often studied as a foreign language in the European Union by 18% of schoolchildren, followed by French 32%, German by 18%, and Spanish by 8%. In the EU, a large fraction of population reports being converse to some extent in English language, where the people communicate in certain language with their own tongue. Among non-English speaking countries, a large percentage of the population claimed to be able to converse in English in the Netherland (87%), Sweden (85%), Denmark (83%), Luxemburg (66%), Finland (60%), Slovenia (56%), Austria (53%), Belgium (52%) and Germany (51%). Norway and Iceland also have a large majority of competent English speakers. In addition, among the younger generations in the mentioned countries, competence in English approaches 100%.

English came to be the language of the legal system, higher education, administrative network, science and technology, trade and commerce. Either the indigenous language was not equipped for these roles and English provided for a convenient vocabulary, or because the use of English was considered prestigious and powerful. English became gradually a major tool for acquiring knowledge, it has come to represent modernization and development and as a link language. It has acquired international roles over the years. It is a matter of statistical fact that English is the most important world language. It is the language of modernity, of the twenty first century. The language of most advanced technologies, air traffic, computing, telecommunications, and language of world politics, diplomacy and international finance.

Books, magazines and newspapers written in English are available in many countries around this world. It is also most commonly language in science world. In 1997 science citation Index reported that 95% of its articles were written in English, even though only half of them came from authors in English speaking countries. English as an international language is intercultural. The use of English and any other language is always culture bound, but the language itself is not bound to any specific culture and political system. In English as foreign language specific varieties of English and specific cultures can be dealt with. This may not be considered valid for English as international EIL. It is clear that in teaching of EIL, the goal cannot be knowledge of details of a given variety or culture or even numbers of these. The ways of speaking and pattern of discourse are different across cultures. Americans may speak English natively yet may not be properly understood by a Briton. A native English speaking Australian may have similar problems with an American or an Indian. In fact English is an exceptional natural language able to obtain international appreciation.

English as international language refers to functions of English not to the given form of the language. Thus it is concerned with the use of English by people of different nations and different cultures in order to communicative with one another. It is conventionally or conceptually different from basic English. It differs from English for special purposes [ESP] as well as in the sense that it is not limit to any specific domain or field. As there are many varieties of English, EIL is an intervarietal way of communication. The listener can be any speaker of English native or non- native. In addition, experience points out the learner's need to prepare for understanding intervarietal spoken English in face to face interactions.

As far as spoken English is concerned, Received Pronunciation [RP] may no longer be considered the ultimate model. The acquisition of native like accent is no longer the ultimate objective of the majority of learners. This assumption has also been asserted by many researchers since language pedagogy is taking a more positive than it did in the past of the existence of varieties of language, dialects and sociolects within a speech of community.

As a lingua-franca of the past century and the new millennium, English is one of the most important means for acquiring access to the world's intellectual of professional & technical resources. Though it may be due to vestige of British colonies or sigh of American cultural imperialism, English is now seen less as a symbol of imperialism and more as a viable candidate for the world's most important international level. At this point in the worlds' history, English is the pre eminent language of wider communication. It is rightly used as a library language, as the medium of science, technology and international trade.

It is a contact language between nation and a part of nation, like it is the only force to bring world together. Language has a very important social purpose, because it is mainly for linguist communication. It is quite possible without use of language.

 Example— A dog barks and informs its masters of approach to a strange.

A child cries and informs its mother that he is hungry, thirsty or uncomfortable with other.

A language can be used in two ways for the purposes of communication as spoken or written, i.e., why the medium of speech is more important rather than the medium of writing. In present condition when India has attained freedom, English is playing very crucial role in the progress of the country in the field of Science& Technology, Management & Economics, Medical, Law, Media, Arts & Crafts, Entertainment etc. the students are most favored engineers, mangers, doctors, lawyers, actors and various experts of their field in European and American countries, because of they could understand or communicate well in English language. The names of Indian students in Information Technology, space science, management, law, and medicine are worldwide recognized. They could acquire the knowledge and expertise in the respective fields in English language. The study of English language is very necessary to introduce us into the fat developing world. If India has to keep pace with the developed nation in present scenario of globalization and liberalization, we must give due importance to the learning of English language. If India has to keep abreast with other fast moving nations of the world, in the field of literature, science, space technology, computer or Information science & Technology, Economics we can't ignore the importance of learning English as a language of universe.

New English is an attempt to rationalize English spellings, to ensure that the written words confirms to spoken words. A framework of rules is proposed; using which there is a fair chance that spelling mistakes are almost impossible. Further, this has been formulated without introduction of any new alphabets or signs. So that the present keyboard of typewriter or computer would suffice to write spellings a proposed in new English. A detailed glossary in alphabetical order is presented covering most of the commonly used words in the English language. Even if there were to be any local or regional differences regarding some pronunciations, even then, the principles enunciated can still be of use to achieve the desired objective.

Language Ideology:

   In sociolinguistics and linguistic anthropology, a language or linguistic ideology is a systematic construct about how particular ways of using languages carry or are invested with certain moral, religious, social, and political values, giving rise to implicit assumptions that people have about a language or about language in general. Common types of language ideology are Standard Language Ideologies, the belief that language homogeneity is beneficial to society, such as that expressed by the English-only movement in the United States. Invested in the Holy Quran, classical Arabic is a good example of language ideology in which it has been always correlated with Islamic practices. In general, differing social speech styles are judged as aspects of social identity and status.

Hence, language ideologies involve interpretations and judgments about vocabulary, grammar, accent, and other vocal features used by speakers. Written language practices are also shaped by language ideologies, as can be seen in the many socialists that develop online.

Language ideology refers specifically to the perceptions held by people about language and, more importantly, how those perceptions are projected onto speakers. University of Michigan Professor of Anthropology Judith Irvine defines a language ideology as "the cultural system of ideas about social and linguistic relationships, together with their loading of moral and political interests". Walt Wolfram and Natalie Schilling-Estes define language ideology as "ingrained, unquestioned beliefs about the way the world is, the way it should be, and the way it has to be with respect to language". This includes assumptions about the merits of homogeneous language within a society, the perceived beauty of certain languages, whether certain languages or dialects are seen as intelligent or unintelligent, and other notions about the value of certain ways of speaking. These aspects are all studied in the field of sociolinguistics, but the idea of language ideology is a relatively recent area of inquiry, which is primarily explored in linguistic anthropology.

The study of language ideology is important to many fields of research, including anthropology, sociology, and linguistics. Especially now that anthropology rejects the idea that culture or cultures represent homogeneous isolated entities, language ideology has become a useful model for understanding how human groups are organized, despite cleavages in belief and practice. For example, multiple languages are spoken in any given human society. Therefore a theory of linguistics that regards human societies as monolingual would be of limited use. Instead, speakers of different languages or dialects may share certain beliefs, practices, or conflicts involving a language, set of languages, or language in general. That is to say, speech communities may be regarded as "organizations of diversity", with language ideologies providing that organization.

Perhaps one of the most common ways that language ideologies are overtly expressed is when parents, teachers or other authorities suggest corrections to speech practices. Such metapragmatic commentary reveals values attached to particular linguistic forms, as well as the judgments about how people should use language in society. Concepts about the effects of language vary widely among social groups and correct use of speech acts, politeness, or phonology acceptance of these values, although this is usually not fully conscious.

Standard Language Ideology – As defined by Rosina Lippi-Green, Standard Language Ideology is "a bias toward an abstract, idealized homogeneous language, which is imposed and maintained by dominant institutions and which has as its model the written language, but which is drawn primarily from the spoken language of the upper middle class". This represents a belief in standard, uniform way of speaking, which is thought to be a better way of communicating, and also that this is the normal way that language exists. As James W. Tollefson notes, however, "linguists agree that variation is normal and intrinsic to all spoken language, even to standard varieties". Thus the idea that a standard language, such as Standard American English, has homogenous phonology is an idealization, based not on the reality of the language, but instead on the ideas about what language should be.

A current example of language ideology in action would be the debate in the United States over Spanish speaking immigrants. The political justifications for an official language in the U.S. are based on the embedded principles described by both language ideology and nationalistic ideology.

While Spanish-speaking immigrants' use of heritage language is currently seen as a problem in the United States, at the same time middle class English speakers are encouraged to learn foreign languages, including Spanish. According to Pomerantz, language ideologies in the US "function to construct expertise in Spanish as a resource for the professional advancement of middle and upper-middle class foreign language learners, while simultaneously casting it as a detriment to the social mobility of heritage language users, i.e., U.S. Latinos".

These assumptions are reinforced by the way that language is taught, through the use of textbooks, dictionaries and grammar lessons.

Implication:

Language ideology has wide implications for society including moral and political assumptions about how to best deal with language in society, and thus for a polities' language policy.

Standard Language Ideologies often negatively affect the ability of minority language speakers to succeed in education because the teacher's perception of what constitutes proper language, and therefore intelligence, could be biased against the language or dialect spoken by the student. One possible example of the effect that standard language ideology has on everyday life in modern America is "linguistic profiling." John Baugh, the inventor of the term "linguistic profiling" has determined that many people can recognize the caller's ethnic dialect on the phone, and if the voice is identified as African-American or Mexican-American, the caller might be subject to racial discrimination.

Chapter-5

<u>Importance of Communicative Approach in Professional and Technical Courses:</u>

The sudden realization by the Gurus of Management and Technocrats, that communication is a critical element of life has given rise to a new concept for language studies. The term communicative English assumes to provide students of professional and Technical education its relevance for meaningful purposes in day to day life. The pattern of English teaching and learning in India since a long period of time has been traditional in nature. The purposes of teaching English in the past aimed to get the students acquainted with the texts which have something to convey. This traditional method of English studies was meant to learn things in orderly to communicate it for the teachers who are already know the information. Since here our concern was associated with assessment, we tried to provide all the information in a sophisticated and ornamental language for impression. But in the present set up where without English we feel helpless, we need to acquire it with little effort. In the past, the technocrats as well as professionals used to feel that study of English was of no value for them. They considered it to be an unnecessary burden. But now it has been realized by established technocrats and business schools guys that success in life is almost impossible without communicative skill. In fact, they realize that in the matter of success in life as well as in business, their so-called hard skills count only fifteen percent of their estimated play while the rest attribute to soft skills. These professional encouraged new phenomena towards the study of language, which gained immense importance with the growth in IT sector. The term "communicative English" has taken hold because of revolution in IT sector. The new technology through internet as well as E-mail has given a digital shape to our language. Perhaps the technocrats in this profession momentarily feel that they need only the vernaculars for their communication needs. One of the basic features of their communication exhibits emphasis on use of plain language. But when they get exposed towards world community of technocrats, they realize the strange burden of lingual simplicity.

The purpose of communication being to convey messages, information or ideas to someone in such a way that he may understand same does not subscribe to mastery over the language. Moreover, communicative English upholds an ideal of using plain or simple language. An organization is a place where people are working at different levels; they all have their own opinions and approaches. In today's world of technical advancement a lot of importance is given to effective communication skills. The dominance of English in administrative world is still there and therefore we have to focus on our attention on conversation in English in India. So, English is rightly a language of professional and technocrats. A successful business always remembers to follow these tips.

To assume difference until similarity is proved.

To initiate communication.

To improve his habit of listening patiently.

To make complete use of his body language to show respect to the other cultures.

To communicate from the receivers points of view.

To learn the art of tolerating a misunderstood of ambiguous statement.

To don't from impression through dress of appearance.

To indentify his own cultural bias.

To be flexible in adjusting with other cultures.

To emphasize the similarities between both cultures.

To communicate with the individual and not the stereotype.

To be situational in direct communication.

To access feedback provided by the recipient.

Each profession has a register and thus a culture of its own.

UK and US are two English –speaking countries but at several instance their registers follow different words for the same thing. For example, in the US it is an apartment for a flat in UK and elevator for a lift in UK.The US-UK language barrier is not a difficult one but one has to really work hard to break the barriers of language where English is spoken as a second language.

The situation at present is that the better you can communicate your ideas, through, experiences and percentage the easier it is to success in life. A person being unable to express himself appears to be in the most difficult and frustrating situation. With the increasing need of physical movement and information sharing;

Communication is becomes a basic necessity of life Expressive maneuverability makes a man adaptive and accommodative to new situation arise out of human movement due to increasing need of overseas jobs.

Actually there is no short-cut formula for good communication. To be a good communicator a person has to acquire sound commands over vocabulary. Besides this he must always have his perceptive since wide open towards the ever-changing world in and around. Effective communication is not a synonym to how many words or expression one may use. It rather implies to what words and expressions one select while communicating.

The language used for communication always plays a vital role.

It necessarily doesn't reflect that one need to make use of needs. The first and foremost objective of communication is to make the receiver understand. The purpose of communication is not to confuse the audience, but to make the receiver accept our information in such a way that he suspends his disbelief and being to accept our view with some regards. Therefore, its objective being to express in a linear way or in a straightforward manner, it becomes a essential to acquire a set of composite skills, one of which is grammatical competence.

ORAL

1. Telephone.

2. Massage

3. Face To face discussion.

4. Intercom.

5. Meeting

6. Presentation.

7. Seminar.

8. Conference.

9. Symposium.

10. Gossip.

WRITTEN

1. Report.

2. Memo.

3. Staff News Letter.

4. Graph/ Chart .

5. Minutes .

6. E-mail.

7. Fax .

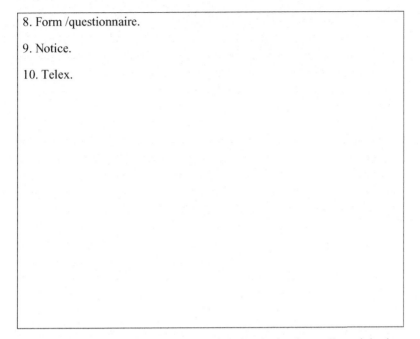

8. Form /questionnaire.

9. Notice.

10. Telex.

Every individual after, several years of study of school or college, inherits a basic knowledge of grammar of English language. But with that naturally acquire knowledge it appears to be very difficult to use the language fluent while speaking or writing. It may be either because of grammar fatigue or lack of communicative skill, both these requirement can be fulfilled, but for achieving this one need to make some conscious, sincere and streamlined efforts. It doesn't mean that one should get on with the books of English grammar for structuring sentence. Since our purpose is to make use of language. We need to emphasize on the communicative part of english grammar. Actually the basic feature of communicative approach is to enhance the capability of student is using as well as understanding the spoken as well as written language. Spoken and written English do not have different grammars, but for such different purpose the same matrix is require to be use differently in real time and transitory , Whereas written English consumes time for its production and becomes a permanent record . While speaking, we try our best to convey our ideas in order to be understood at once. Here neither the communicator nor the audience gets times to revise. While writing not only does the writer get time to revise and rewrite, but the reader also gets the chance to re- read and analyze the version. A written word is an orphan because its meaning is subject to interpretation. But a spoken word is legitimate the speaker is there to protect it meaning. Perhaps it may be one of the reasons for which people in power never write they only speak. The spoken word has the metaphysics of presence. Hence it is more authentic then written word. Therefore, it becomes essential on the part of a person trying to communicate some-thing to choose the situations. Another basic point that should be taken note of is that, before communicating it becomes essential on the part of a person trying to communicate some-thing to choose the situations. Another basic point that should be taken note of is that, before communicating it becomes necessary to know 'what to communicate'. Simply knowing what to communicate will not serve the whole purpose. Besides knowing this one must also be aware of the audience to whom he is going to communicate and how it is to be communicated. Over and above all it must be guided by why to communicate.

A young technocrat or professional may get puzzled because never before was it through that the skill of communication as so important: but now it is time for them to realize the fact that if they ignore to develop their skills of communication, they cannot have a commanding personality, since communication has a social parameter, one needs to acquire it for upholding one's integrity. Since the scope of these professionals is not limited to any boundary, it becomes for them to acquire the skill of communicating in English, which is the world language. To meet the demands of industry as well as the society communication skill is as valuable as social behaviour. One of the most important things to remember is that everyone can improve, but for this one has to make a conscious effort. To be a good speaker, one has to be a good listener. Spoken communication needs organization of ideas and thoughts before delivery.

In order to enhance the power of communication one must keep the following thing in mind;

➤ Think before you start speaking.

➤ Realize the message you want to convey.

➤ Try to make it easier for the listener to remember your view, by getting on to the point quickly.

➤ Visualize the outcome of your conversation in a positive manner.

➤ Make efforts to persuade your audience to accept your point of view.

➤ Have a plan in your mind about what you want to speak or what you want to achieve.

➤ Try to have some knowledge about the acceptability perception.

Fear or nervousness is to some extent obstacles for the beginners trying to communicate in English. After all the purpose of a particular conversation or communication is to make your idea or message accepted by the throughout in communicative language. It is better to emphasize on the major points of your topic. If possible try to provide a suitable and familiar examples relating to your topic in order to make the conversation more interesting. As far as practicable clarify your message by delivering deep into the issues. Finally frame tactful questions for the listener or audience to get the feedback, either positive or negative. Otherwise your communication remains incomplete. One thing that is to be kept in mind is that everyone may not agree with your views or ideas. So, if you get a contrary feedback instead of taking it as a rejection, you should accept it as a new response. In order to develop such attitude there are few points to be taken into consideration, which may add something extra into your personality an inter-personal skill:

❖ Be direct in your approach.

❖ Be positive about your communicative skills.

❖ Avoid mental stress and be comfortable

❖ Develop a list of positive affirmations showing that what you want already exists.

❖ Let yourself feel the joy of success.

❖ Have respect for others.

❖ Try to avoid words that hurt.

❖ Be good in manners for establishing a rapport.

❖ Be flexible in order to have control of the conversation.

❖ Process your ideas, feelings and information in such a way that you can find agreement.

❖ Try to eliminate negative feelings.

❖ Keep smiling and occasionally "poke fun" at yourself.

❖ Be friendly.

With these things in mind we must try to have two more important things for better communication, sensitivity for acquiring information and clarity for better expression. When we are communicating our expression creates an effect in the mind of our audience. We can put it like this; the language we use creates a kind of stimuli or responses in the mind of audience. If we are unable to make people respond to our views and thoughts then our communication becomes incomplete. Therefore, the study of language becomes a matter of paramount importance. It makes us know what to speak or how to speak.

Importance of Communication

An organization is a place where people are working at different levels. They all have their own opinions and approaches. For a common profit all the different people must join hands together. In today's world of technical advancement a lot of importance is given to effective communication skills.

The dominance of English in the administrative world is still prevalent and therefore we have to focus our attention conversation in English in India.

Hence we can say that English is a language of technocrats, professionals, and the twenty first century man, riding the crest of great technological and scientific advancement has started experiencing formidable changes in the means or modes of communication. This phenomenon has been variously described as microelectronic or the communication or information revolution. Its impact on the society has been regarded as analogous to the impact into railways had on mid-nineteenth century. As a matter of fact, all technological changes affect the style and shape of life in societies. These also influence on the courses of communication which ultimately stamp their effects on English language.

In fact, English enjoys a commanding position in science, engineering, law, medicine, commerce, industries and diplomatic services. The importance of English at the official level is well known. English is the associate language at the central, states that have adopted their regional languages for official business. India is a land of many languages, cultures and religions.

The future of English in India is really bright: ---

➢ A learner and learning centered approach move from teaching to learning.

➢ A communicative and task based approach with authentic communication tasks and learning tasks.

➢ Emphasis on learning to learn or encouraging creativity.

➢ ESP in higher classes' better preparation for work or study tasks.

➢ More intensive use of the modern language in the classroom developing language awareness.

➢ Use of information technology or multi-media etc.

➢ Encouraging learner autonomy, self- assessment and cross-cultural awareness.

➢ Project or assignment work for the betterment.

The single most important observation is that the objective of communication is not the reception. The whole preparation, presentation and content of a speech must be geared to the audience. The presentation of a perfect project plan is a failure, if audience does not understand or are not persuaded its merits. A customer's tour is a waste of time, if he or she leaves without realizing full worth of your product. The objective of communication is to make your message understood and remembered. The theme is that communication education is vital to the development of whole person.

The result is rather break of communication or miscommunications, while instead of solving problems, often create new ones at the technological, professional, social and cultural levels. In a multilingual country like India, English is lingua-franca through which future citizens, who are being groomed in the technical or professional and vocational English language, are going to discuss and sort out the problems of the society. The professional as a whole in the shared system of symbols, beliefs, attitudes, values, expectations norms for behaviour are the communicative style of this society. The personality development and interpersonal skills play a very vital role in each and every aspect of life, whether it is personal or professional. Thus awareness of English language among the technocrats and professional to the fact as to how communicative skills, language studies form an integral part of teaching, research and development in technical as well as professional studies. Through re-discover the newer methods of English language laboratory by making experimentations on pronunciation practice, phonetics and linguistics.

This study reveals that business students underestimate how much of their time may be spent in meeting, the importance of international communication skills, how often they may have to interact with other employees, the importance of oral presentations and ability to use multimedia technology. A more realistic awareness of the importance of these skills might motivate students to prepare more carefully for their communication lives in the workplace.

Communication education is fundamental to career success and the entire business enterprise. People entering the workforce are assisted by communication skills and employers endorse communication skills as basic to most jobs. Communicative skill is essential in multiple professional careers including accounting, auditing, banking, engineering, industrial hygiene, information science, public relation and sales&purchase.

Upward mobility is more probable as communications skills upgrade or the idea generate on language culture. Business and customer interactions are more satisfying and productive with the development of communication skills. Communication skills are essential to those in human resource development, with both business executives and entrepreneurs benefit from communication education. Good communication skills are becoming a requirement for almost any job, that corporate leaders or human resource managers are realizing the importance of strong interpersonal communication skills to performance of all employees, not just those in supervisory and managerial positions. Engineers can relate the same theories of mathematics, mechanics and technology, but the modern engineer must also be able to communicate effectively in a shared tongue. English has become the ascendant language internationally, being the most widespread. This will influence the language of communication between professionals and technocrats at the international platform. In this age of globalization, a number of international projects in technical or professional are increased and cross-cultural communication or collaboration is on rise. English is cited as the major language of international business, diplomacy, science and management. It is through this method that English appears to be spreading most, compared to past centuries that were dominated by immigration and settlement, such as Canada, USA, Australia, UK and Africa. English is the prime means of communication and can often same as the global language between two people from two different cultures, wherein English is not a native tongue. In the other words it is a pre-requisite for success and for these communicative skills plays an important role. Effective communicative is a short-cut to distinction; this communication gives us an edge over others. It is a communication, which makes people successful and brings them to lime light. There is any group of people or any professional it is mainly the communication, which has given them the distinct edge. Whether the successful businessman, student, engineer, doctor, officers, or politicians etc. or any person, who are doing the by the use of certain communicative English. The purposes of teaching English language in the past aimed to get the students acquainted with the texts which have something to convey. But in the present setup where without English it feels helpless, one needs to acquire it with little effort. These professional encouraged new phenomena towards study of language, which gained immense importance with the growth of IT sector, Telecom sector, Management sector, Media sector etc. the importance of communicative language as communicative English has taken hold because of the revolution in the IT sector and in Management sector. The socio-linguistic study shows that English language is a form of human social behaviour either in technical or in professional institutions. Language reflects the difference between technical or professional communities, which split up the group and each group displays differences of behaviour. The primary function of language is to convey ideas one person to another, but these ideas may be information forward or request in the form of scientific, geographical, economic, psychological, technical, vocational, legal and social. Language being extends and common medium communicative method of education aims at simplifying tings at linguistic level so as to make things coherent. Further cogency of thought or expression is achieved various interactive methods of putting the content in order to acquaint the learner like technical or professional with the basics.

How language use in multilingual and multicultural India is naturally diverse. It is rightly chips in that technical field and language both are intricately interlined and brings forth the latent personality in the students of professional or technical education. The pre-requisites of presentation of our national talents as professionals or technical skills are well in communication skills and proper interaction. A majority of students prefer to read it as a language and an effective means of self expression. Therefore, there is a steady demand for English language in the college of management, engineering, medical, law or other vocational courses. The student can be encouraged by expression them need of the language and arranging extempore, debate, group-discussion, personality development, gossip, reading news paper, magazines, writing articles or fiction in English language to get more command over the language. It dreams the impact of English language for the personal development in professional or technical students have needs for daily life. Language is not only a phenomenon; it is a creation of human social needs, wants and demands. Hence human being depend on language as they depend on air, water, food, sex,cloths and the universe around it for their own existence. The language is extremely complex and highly versatile codes that use to communicate our thoughts, desires, experiences, ideas, notions and observation to other persons. Language and human culture are intimately related and one is indispensable to other. When the person's attention is turning increasingly towards analyzing his or her culture, it is natural that they should attempt to examine in detail the means of communication, which is essential to the family or their society. It holds the view that recent years have shown an explosion of interest in using computers for English, learning or teaching. However, with the availability of multimedia computing and Internet, the role of computers in English language instruction to the "Low English Proficient" [LEP], students has now become and own important issue for large number of English language professionals and technocrats throughout the world.

In the meanwhile, English as a language of communication has acquired a distinct status on its own right. It has a medium transplanted from outside as an adopted language, but as a spontaneous growth within a socio-cultural matrix. Where we may truly belong and seek to fulfill ourselves, by modes of expression and manners of speech. Self expression is the basic motive and within that limit one may seek to ply one's trade, which is to understand and communicate within a congenial psychological climate. The aim is to interpret the condition of man above the barriers of speech and hindrance of geographical boundaries, to project a brighter image of speaker among the chosen couriers of globe.

1. Seek to clarify your ideas before communicating.

2. Examine the true purpose of each communication.

3. Considered the physical and human setting whenever you communicate.

4. Consult others, when appropriate, in planning communication.

5.   Be meaningful, while you communicate, of the over tones as well as the basic content of your message.

6.   Take the opportunity, when it arises, to convey something of help or value to the receiver.

7. Follow of your communication.

8. Communication for tomorrow as well as for today.

9. Be sure your actions support your communication.

10. Seek note only to be understood but to understand as well as be a good listener.

So, communication may be defined as covering all methods of making known or transmitting ideas and information with the object of making oneself understood. This is the act of creating understanding with wisdom or knowledge. Good communication and use effective communication to use as:

'Good' communication means that the party 'B' has understood a concept that party 'A' wished to convey to 'B'. It is a pre-requisite but does not ensure.

'Effective' communication means that the desired result has been obtained. It includes behavioural aspects like persuasion, motivation, coercion and the like.

The Communications structures are human relationship in such a way that a group of people can work together to achieve a goal. Thus communication makes organizational life with possible.

The five C's of communication: - To effective writing comprises the communication with its actual base.

I. Clarity

II. Completeness

III. Consciousness

IV. Correctness

V. Courtesy

VI. Communication

Formal communication skill in interpersonal relations assumes greater importance. The assumptions, view points and feelings of the speaker and the listen will vary depending upon the organizational relationship and the situation.

The communications are not always rational or irrational, because words can be conceal as well as convey ideas. Without effective communication one cannot succeed in maintaining food relations with others, thereby reducing one's chances of success in life.

'Communication', as a scholarly field of study, is a science that produces skilled communication practitioners. It deals with the process of informing, motivating, teaching and entertaining people. It also involves creating and disseminating information, facts, ideas and feelings to its users. Communication has manifold functions of which the main ones include informing, persuading, sharing, socializing, motivating, educating and entertaining the people. These functions are carried art by various means of communication- signs, words, written language, postal services, telephone, radio, television and computers.

Modern information technologies provide inexpensive, fast, capable, reliable means of supporting communication. Networked computer systems like the internet and extranets are the enabling platforms that support communication. Historically, these systems began with the telegraph, the telephone, radio and television. It is only communication which can upgrade the communication skills for employability or the speech of cultural identity.

Importance of the English Language

Language is not a static entity; it changes over time. Changed may be observed in the phonology, syntax and vocabulary of a language. Thus industrialization, colonization, urbanization, migration, the development of mass communication and technological diffusion has some role to play in language change. Language has to be learned new by every generation, and even though we might claim that certain kinds of principles do not have to be learned, because they are innate, enough must be learned so that variation between generations likely to occur.

Language varies according to the age of the person using it, sex and occupation. Accepted patterns exist for communicating between and within the generations. Old people to young, young to old, parents to children, children to parents, adolescent to their peers and so on. Language used in addressing men and women varies subtly, we can compliment a men on a new necktie with the words what a pretty tie that is! But not with how pretty you look today! It is an expression reserved for complimenting a woman.

The occupation of a person causes his language to vary, particularly on the use he makes of technical terms. Teachers, soldiers, doctors, engineers, managers, lawyers and even those of the criminal underworld have their special vocabularies. People is one location often speak a language differently from speakers somewhere else. A language is a systematic means of communication by the use of sounds or conventional symbols. It is a code that we all use to express ourselves and communicate to others. It is a communication by words of mouth; it is mental faculty or power of vocal communication. It is a system for communicating ideas and feelings using sounds, gestures, signs or marks. Any means of communicating ideas, human speech, and the expression of ideas by the voice and sounds articulated by the organs of throat or mouth is a language. A language is the written and spoken methods of combining words to create meaning used by a particular group of people. Language, so far as we know, is something specific to humans, that is to say it is the basic capacity that distinguishes humans from all other living beings. Language therefore remains potentially a communicative medium capable of expressing ideas and concepts as well as moods, feelings and attitudes. A set of linguists who based their assumptions of language on psychology made claims that language is nothing but habit formation. According to them, language is learnt through use, through practice. In their view, the more one is exposed to the use of language, the better one learns. Written languages use symbols characters to build words. The entire sets of words are the language's vocabulary. The ways in which the words can be meaningfully combined is defined by the language's syntax or grammar. The actual meaning of words and combinations words is defined by the language's semantics.

The latest and the most advanced discoveries and inventions in science and technology are being made in the universities located in the United States of America, where English language is the means of scientific discourse. The historical circumstances of India having been ruled by the British for over two centuries have given the Indians an easy access to mastering English language and innumerable opportunities for advancement in the field of science and technology. Many Indians have become so skilled in English language and have won many international awards for creative or comparative literatures during the last few years. Something ago, an Indian author, Arundhati Roy won the prestigious Booker Prize for her book, "The God of Small Things".

Over the years, English language has become one of our principal assets in getting a global leadership for books written by Indian authors and for films made by Indians in English language. A famous Indian moviemaker Shekhar Kapoor's film 'Elizabeth', has got several nominations for Oscar awards. It does not require any further argument to establish the advantage English language has brought to us at international level. English language comes to our aid in our commercial transactions throughout the globe. English is a language of the latest business management in the world and Indian proficiency in English has brought laurels to many Indian business managers. English is a means not only for international commerce; it has become increasingly essential for inter-state commerce and communication.

In India, people going from North to South for education or business mostly communicate in English, which has become a link language. Keeping this in mind, the parliament has also recognized English as an official language in addition to Hindi. All the facts of history and developments in present day India underline the continued importance of learning English in addition to vernaculars. Some of the states of India are witnessing popular increase in public demand for teaching of English language from the primary classes. The great demand for admission in English medium schools throughout the country is a testimony to the attraction of English to the people of India. Many of the leaders, who denounce English, send their own children to English medium schools. Many of the schools in the country have English as the sole or additional medium of instruction. A language attracts people because of the wealth of literature and knowledge enshrined in it. English poses no danger to Indian languages. The Indian languages are vibrant and are developing by the contributions of great minds using them as their vehicle of expression. English is available to us as a historical heritage in addition to our own language. We must make the best use of English to develop ourselves culturally and materially, so that we can compete with the best in the world of mind and matter. English language is our window to the world, where anyone can excel their idea with the values of work.

English language is one tool to establish our viewpoint.

We can learn from others experience.

We can check the theories of foreigners against our experience.

We can reject the untenable and accept the tenable.

We can also propagate our theories among the international audience and readers.

We can make use of English to promote our worldwide and spiritual heritage throughout the globe. Swami Vivekananda established the greatness of Indian view of religion at the world conference of religions in Chicago in 1893. He addressed the gathering in impressive English. Many spiritual gurus have since converted thousands of English people to our spirituality by expressing their thought or ideas in masterful English. English has thus become an effective means of promoting Indian view of life, and strengthening our cultural identity in this world.

When William Caxton setup his printing press in London (1477), the new hybrid language, vernacular English mixed with courtly French and scholarly Latin became increasingly standardized and by 1611, when the authorized king James version of the Bible was published, the educated English of London had become core of what is now called standard English. By the time of Johnson's dictionary (1755) and in American declaration of Independence (1776), English was an international or recognizable as the language we use today. The orthography of English was more or less established by 1650 and in England in particular, a form of standard educated speech known as Received Pronunciation (RP) spread from major public schools in the 19th century. This ascent was adopted in the early 20th century by the British Broadcasting Corporation (BBC) for its announcers and readers or variously known as RP, BBC English, Oxford English and the King's or Queen's English.

Generally, Standard English today does not depend on ascent but rather on shared educational experiences, mainly of the printed language. Present day English is an immensely varied language, having absorbed material from many other tongues. It is spoken by more than 300 million native speakers and between 400 and 800 million foreign users. It is the official language of air transport and shipping, the leading language of science, technology, computers and commerce, a major medium of education, publishing or international negotiation. English in India is no more the language of the alien rulers, but it has been accepted as an Indian language and by Sahitya Academy since 1960. People of different regional languages can exchange their thoughts and ideas through English or benefit by it. In this respect, communicative English plays a very important role in India. Now a lot of books are being translated from various regional languages into English. The exchange of thoughts through English will definitely help broaden the horizon of literature as a whole. But unless English that is used in translation is communicative, the objective of translation will be defeated. On the whole, the art of writing, reading or speaking should be like a window of plain glass through which the writer, reader or speaker's meaning becomes clearly visible. In the first it was due to the efforts of Lord Macaulay, that English language was first introduced in schools or colleges as a medium of instruction. Language and communication skills especially in English are recognized as important element in education of modern generation. Yet there seems to be limited implementation of English courses globally, despite its lingua-franca status. Those institutions that have already impempted multi-lingual and communication elements will be at the forefront of providing the demands of industry or society. The importance of English language in the professional education is recognized all over the world. The globalization directly influences the industry's needs; a global citizen must be able to easily cross national and cultural boundaries'. This in turn directly affects education, so a common code for communication is required. Those educational institutions, which meet the language requirements for the new global market, which will have bright prospects in the new millennium.

Chapter-6

Impact of Social and Technological changes

Language has been an ever growing and ever changing phenomenon, changing under the impact of social and technological changes or the users of language have always been adapting to the effective, optimum use of language, be it with the help of language laboratories or learning in the classroom or trying it in different kinds of media.

There have been many reasons causing changes in grammar syntax, vocabulary and pronunciation. We have no time and space to discuss all the reasons for linguistic changes. But one reason that we cannot fail to take notice is various kinds of technological change that have linguistic changes. We can identify two kinds of technological change that one let us do the same things more quickly and cheaply. The other leads us to different things and perhaps even to become works did in some way different people. The revolution in spinning and weaving technology around A.D., 1800 for example, brought great economic change in Europe and North America but did not bring a comparable social revolution. On the other hand rail, road, airplane did affect profoundly our notions of time, distance and travel or brought structural changes in commercial and residential use of space. Telegraph service and typewriters made business communication more efficient, telephones brought new kinds of interactions, not simply greater speed. In the twentieth century the advent of space, exploration, technologies and satellites, the coming of computers, cybernetics and other microelectronic devices have revolutionized and almost changed human civilization and its communication systems. The recent technological transformation ushering in a new "Information Society" has introduced 'Cyberpunk' or 'Cyborg' and an endless variety of concepts the communication of which expressly demands a new handling of language.

The scientific and technological advancements also make major contribution towards enriching the language by bringing in a flood of new words produced by the scientific necessities. The sixteenth century had introduced especially words to do with the human body, like skeleton, tibis, abdomen and tendon and also a number of diseases like catarrah, epilepsy, mumps and smallpox. In seventeenth century too, the scientific words were predominantly medical and biological i.e., vertebra, tonsil, pneumonia, lumbago, but there were also quite a few new words in chemistry including acid, in physics i.e., including formula of logarithm and series. In the eighteenth century came enormous expansion in the vocabulary of biological sciences, for this was the great age of biological description and classification. From this period came many of the descriptive terms of Zoology or Botany, like albino, coleopteran, anther, fauna, dicotyledon, habitat, pistil and so on. The great changes in chemical theory in the late eighteenth century also produced many new words including hydrogen, oxygen, nitrogen and molecule.

Engineer, technologists, managers and scientists have the challenge of making a vehicle for communicating efficiently, and with ease and plainness, the new concepts and ideas of a new era. Linguists in general and the teachers or students of engineering or management colleges have new grounds to tread in preparing human resources to carry on the burden of ever expanding new knowledge of the twenty first century. In the mean while, English as language of communication has acquired a distinct status on its own right, not as medium transplanted from out-side as an adopted language. But it is such as a spontaneous growth within a social-cultural matrix, by modes of expression and manners of speech. Self-expression is the basic motive and within that limit one may seek to ply one's trade which is to understand and communicate within a congenial psychological climate. English has become one of the major languages of the world today. It has occupied an important status in country too. In every walk of Indian life, English plays a vital role whether political, social, economic or cultural, its acts as a window to knowledge. It was believed and expected that English would soon go forever with the departure of the white people from our country, but it has struck such deep roots in the Indian soil that it is read, written or spoken on a large scale in India even today. The acceptability of English got a severe jolt in 1967, when students in the north agitated for the removal of foreign language from this country. But with the passage of time English language came back with a bang and this age of globalization the knowledge of English appears to be a key to success in practical life. And much of this work has received international acclaim with recognition. Even the most important newspapers, magazines, books, journals, souvenirs or other articles in this country are those, which employ

English as their medium. For effective inter-cultural communication a person has to identify the language barriers and modulate his oral or written skills according to his requirement.

Some of the best method is to improve his or her writing and speaking skills as,

➢ Clarify of expression through concrete words.

➢ Consciousness of words like climb instead of work up.

➢ Correctness in providing information.

➢ Carefully planned and formatted from the reader's point of view.

It is easier to speak in another language than to write. However, one cannot avoid face-to-face conversation. To establish rapport one has to concentrate on verbal as well as non-verbal language. When an Englishman speaks to an ESL speaker, then he/she has to concentrate on:

➢ Clarity of his/her pronunciation by proper emphasis on contextual words.

➢ Feedback provided by the receiver through their body language.

➢ Rephrasing if necessary.

➢ Courtesy to ask "Am I going too fast"? But not "Is this too difficult for you".

➢ Language should include Idioms, fabulous and fantastic words.

➢ Use of foreign phrases for greetings.

➢ Listening to speakers carefully and patiently.

➢ Adapting to the style of the speakers.

That is why writing or speaking of a language is form of expression. The mechanism behind expression is mainly formation of thought or an idea to be transmitted symboligically. Hence symbolical transmission of thought is expression.

By drawing lines: writing –script

By making sound: speaking-speech

By physical movement: gesture and posture

The purpose of the general education requirements is need for the students an appreciation for the acquisition of the knowledge, skills and perspective that constitute the foundation of college and life-long learning, responsible or rewarding professional service, personal development and civic responsibility. General education promotes free and rational inquiry, critical thinking, creative expression, and understanding or respect for diversity, intellectual integrity social responsibility.

The four major areas within the general education requirements include:

1.   Intellectual exploration (IE) for education majors.

A traditional area of university inquires that include Fine-Arts, physical/life science, and social & behaviour science. Lower division writing (WR) ensures students develop the rhetorical skills necessary for success in the writing assignments.

2.   Quantitative Reasoning (QA and QB or QA/QB).

Quantitative reasoning prepares students for an information based society in which the ability to use and critically evaluate information, especially numerical information, is central to the role requirements of an informed citizen.

3.   Communication/Writing (CW) prepares students to speak and write clearly within the standards of practice set by the discipline. It provides students advanced instruction in speaking and writing, so that those skills continue to develop throughout the educational programme.

4. Diversity (DV), this requirement extends cross-cultural understanding, replacing the impulse to stereotype with better informed reasoning, understanding and judgment skills.

Quantitative intensive [QI] promotes further development of quantitative reasoning skills; a deeper understanding of the particular subject matter; substantial application of quantitative, analytical problem solving.

- Child, Adolescent and Human development.

- Ethnic studies, multicultural/multilingual education and effective instructional approach for English language learners.

- Foundations of exceptionality and effective instruction for students with disabilities in inclusive classroom.

Research Education:

Principles of Assessment and data based decision making/behavoiur support.

Use Communicative language and its development.

Reading & writing practice for its foundations and methods.

Integrating educational arts into academic learning for language communication.

Using language technology in diverse classrooms.

English as a Mother-tongue language

English language over the last thousand years has borrowed words from three hundred fifty other languages in this world. The language is a system of conventional signals used for communication by a whole community. Like language is a very important means of communication between humans.

"A language is a system arbitrary vocal symbol used for human communication." **- Wardaugh, 1972**

Like 'A' can communicate his or her ideas, emotions, believes or feelings to 'B' as they share a common code that makes up the language.

India is country where parochially all those who deal in industry, exports, entertainment, finance can speak English and transact all business, letters,reports,drafts, negotiation, contracts in English. The investors are amazed that most of Indian workers with a small exception can learn English world easily and follow the engineering drawing to the salt detail and produce the parts as well.

A Communicative Approach in English

Communication is an important aspect of human behaviour, communication has been important from the time of Adam and Eve. Over the years it has been refined and made into a sophisticated tool. Etymologically, the word communication is derived from the Latin root 'Communis'; which means transmitting information sharing of information or intelligence. The most common medium of communication is language. While speaking us often resort to physical gestures we wave our hands, shrug our shoulders, smile and nod to reinforce what we say. Besides, there are several other means of communication available to us. We use non-linguistic symbols such as traffic lights, road signs, railway signals to convey information relating to the movement of vehicles and trains. We also use telegraphic code for quick transmission of message and secret code for communicating defense and other highly confidential information. For communication all these codes are valid in their special frames of reference.

Keith Davis, defines communication as; "Communication is the process by which information is transmitted between individual and organizations, so that an understanding response results." The transfer of information and understanding from one person to another person, it is a way of reaching others with facts, ideas, thoughts and values. It is a bridge of meaning among people so that they can share what they feel and know. By using this bridge a person can cross safely the river of misunderstanding that sometimes separates people. It is a process, the components and their relationships are sender, message, channel, receiver and response.

Business Communication

Language is a common symbol system which use for sharing our experience with others. The purpose of all communication i.e., speaking, writing, sending a message to another person is to elicit action. The activities succeed or fail and our goals are achieved or not achieved, according to our ability to communicate effectively with others.

Business activities are two types:-

Internal – Among the internal activities are maintaining and improving the morale of employees, giving orders to workers, prescribing method and procedures, announcing policies and organizational changes and keeping the management informed.

External – The activities relate to selling and obtaining goods and services, reporting to the government and the shareholders on the financial condition and business operations and creating a favourable for conducting business.

Every organization held together by communication. It makes for better relationship and understanding between boss and subordinate, colleagues, people within the organization and outside it. Communication is central to everything that we do. It plays a pivotal role in development, especially today in the context of globalization. People are different and we need to understand the nature of those differences and try to modify our interpersonal behaviour to cope with them. Communication is effective only when the message is understood and when it stimulates action or encourages the receiver to think in new ways. The success of information passing depends very much on the nature and quality of the information received and this in turn depends on the nature or quality of the relationship between the persons involved.

Every organization has an informal communication network called as the "Grapevine" that supplements official channels. This informal channel carries unofficial information about the management's policies and plans, work programmes, the company's performance, individual managers and such matters related to the companies. Many employees rely on the grapevine as their main source of information about the organization. Information gained through informal channels may be inaccurate; it needs to be skillfully controlled because it can influence the efficiency of the organization. Therefore, the main purpose of every communication in business is to obtain some result that is to secure an action by the receiver. The sender expects him to do something on receiving the message that write a cheque, place an order, approve an action, send some information etc. to achieve this purpose the language used is direct, plain, and concise and to the point, the style concentrates on drawing attention, arousing interest or creating desire, developing conviction and inducing action. The main features that lend business communication a distinct identity are as follows:

➤ It deals with various commercial and industrial subjects.

➤ It is characterized by certain formal elements such as commercial and technical vocabulary, the use of graphic and audio-visual aids and conventional formats.

➤ It is impartial and objective as extreme care is taken to convey information accurately and concisely.

➤ It has comparatively a high concentration of certain complex writing techniques and procedures.

A business communication is using in effective language for conveying a commercial or industrial message to achieve a predetermined purpose.

Universal language may refer to a hypothetical or historical language spoken and understood by all or most of the world's population. In some contexts, it refers to a means of communication said to be understood by all living things, beings, and objects alike. It may be the ideal of an international auxiliary language for communication between groups speaking different primary languages. In other conceptions, it may be the primary language of all speakers, or the only existing language. Some mythological or religious traditions state that there was once a single universal language among all people, or shared by humans and supernatural beings, however, this is not supported by historical evidence.

In other traditions, there is less interest in or a general deflection of the question. For example in Islam the Arabic language is the language of the Quran, and so universal for Muslims. The written classical Chinese language was and is still read widely but pronounced somewhat differently by readers in different areas of China, in Vietnam, Korea and Japan for centuries; it was a de facto universal literary language for a broad-based culture. In something of the same way Sanskrit in Nepal was a literary language for many for whom it was not a mother tongue.

Comparably, the Latin language (qua Medieval Latin) was in effect a universal language of literati in the Middle Ages, and the language of the Vulgate Bible, in the area of Catholicism which covered most of Western Europe and parts of Northern and Central Europe also.

In a more practical fashion, trade languages, as ancient Koine Greek, may be seen as a kind of real universal language, which was used for commerce.

In historical linguistic, monogesis refers to the idea that all spoken human languages are descended from a single ancestral language spoken many thousands of years ago.

Mythological universal languages:

Various religious texts, myths and legends describe a state of humanity in which originally only one language was spoken. In Judeo-Christian beliefs, the "confusion of tongues" described in the Biblical story of the Tower of Babel tells of the creation of numerous languages from an original Adamic language. Similar myths exist in other cultures describing the creation of multiple languages as an act of a god, such as the destruction of a 'knowledge tree' by Brahma in Indic tradition, or as a gift from the God Hermes in Greek myth. Other myths describe the creation of different languages as concurrent with the creation of different tribes of people, or due to supernatural events.

The impact of communication in business, understand the nature, organization, objective and function of business firms. They have various departments or branches and many employees at various levels of management. In spite of individual differences, all must move in the same direction with the same purpose and act in unison for achieving the common goal. Companies have to communicate with outside agencies and other companies, government and private bodies, newspapers, advertisers, manufactures, suppliers, clients and customers etc. But there is also the need to communicate within the company itself, and communication between a superior and subordinate, i.e., from higher to lower levels of authority. In India, because of rapid development of industry and technology, an increasing need has been felt for improving skills of communication at all levels of administration.

So, communication is a range of purposeful behaviour, which is used with intent within the structure of social exchanges, to transmit information, our observation or internal states or to bring about changes in the immediate environment. Verbal as well non-verbal behaviours are included, as long as some intent, evidenced by anticipation of outcome can be inferred. The incorporation of several components of the fundamentals of emotional intelligence in education facilitates advanced communication skills. However, given the traditionalist nature of many engineering, management, medical and law this may take some time before change is evidenced. The incorporation of language and communication improvement courses is an important element of continuous learning and will ultimately contribute to the process of learning. This should in turn facilitate advancements in engineering and indeed education through streaming fundamental communication skills. In the communicative English for technical and professional education, it emphasize on linguistics and phonetics. Software like the oxford talking dictionary and the random house talking dictionary, vocabulary wizard talk it.

Communicative Skills

Personality Development remains incomplete if the communicative skills are ignored. For a technocrat, this is very important to master to reach the pinnacle of success. In fact many problems generate due to poor communication. So, it is very important to identify and the communication barriers mainly psychological, semantic and physical.

Some knowledge on modern grammar is very essential to speak and write flawless English is the lingua-franca in India as well as in many parts of the world. Pronunciation with correct ascent and stress increases the degree of understandability. Words should be dealt with proper care lest they should not change the meaning. This again possible if the professional institutes encourage in establishing language laboratories. Students will then get exposed to many software tools, language modification tools, language correction tools, phonetics recognition tools etc, to train themselves and know their shortcomings and strong points. For the overall development of personality it is very essential. However the guides also play a crucial role here by taking individual care and giving them the best polish to shine forever.

Remember that it is small things in life which matter the most and hurt the most like, we can sit on a mountain and enjoy the serenity but we cannot on a pin. Similarly, in technical education communication is most neglected, as it is considered to be a very small thing, but when a person stumbles in the professional career because of this small thing, it not only hurts but pains. It is absolutely suicidal to ignore communication in technical education. People may be technically strong but unless they communicate it is of no use, it is just a waste. So, professional success depends on twenty percent of technical skills and seventy eight percent of soft skills, the major skill being communication. Even the corporate look for people who have a perfect blend of knowledge and soft skill are also depends upon the communicative English. At Wipro, of the total allocated to training budget forty percent is for soft skills enhancement. Why is that in an organization like Wipro, they need soft skills training. Because success means analyzing and upgrading and to go up the ladder we need soft skills, the major being communication. Hence, if knowledge is food for life, communication is slat and attitude adds flavours. In educational communication, the sources are teachers, institutions and the messages related to the curriculum, the content, the skills and the attitudes and related activities, which educate, inform, train, enlighten, inspire and entertain those students. The receivers are the student and various teaching strategies such as demonstrations, tutorials, textbooks, assignments, audio-visual components, libraries etc. are used as media to transfer the contents. With the advancement in communication technologies, it is now possible to impart education throughout the world via satellites, which have the potential to communicate even live events to the students at their work place. Thus, education has crossed many barriers of space and time. As a consequence, the methods of teaching and learning have also changed. Technologies such as computers, video-tapes, video-dick, tele-texts, communication satellites and tele-conferencing services have steeped in to improve the nature of educational communication. These technologies have made the teaching-learning process more lively and interactive. They have enhanced the pace of learning and also improve the means of retention and retrieval of information. Interestingly, Hills (1986), regards the computer as men 'Fourth –Brain' taking its place alongside the other three like, Cerebrum, Optic Lobes and Cerebellum. A perfect blend of knowledge, skills and attitude is surely going to take you to the pinnacle of success. Communicative method of teaching presupposes a graded pattern of imparting academics, so as to make it learner friendly. Language being the extant and common medium, communicative method of teaching aims at simplifying things at the linguistic level so as to make things coherent. Further, cogency of thought and expression is achieved through various interactive methods of putting the content in order to acquaint the learner with the basics. Communicative method of teaching [CMT] involves an interactive method with emphasis on activity oriented learning instead of teaching as a sort of preaching from a high pedestal.

A communicative method of learning process of its core subjects like;

(1) All the students, teachers, writers, scientist and professionals should be made to improve their communication skills by increasing the language input in them so as to use them in transferring language.

(2) All the textbooks should be collaborative and must associate at least a language expert to simplify the expression to make it attractive, interesting and learner-friendly. They may suggest suitable substitute/alternative words and expression to the contents.

(3) Subject vocabulary should be made compulsory at the end of each chapter of the book, so as to enable the learners to understand the subject matter without the help of experts. Meanings of different words and expressions used in the text must be explained in detail for better understanding.

(4) The textbooks may be re-written to accommodate the extensive use of pictures, flowcharts, models, examples etc. and make the content interactive as well as activity oriented.

(5) The criteria for selection of teachers and authors should be based on the communicative skill apart from their resourcefulness.

(6) Communicative language studies should be open to all subject experts.

(7) At the higher level of studies, curriculum should include some exercises by the learners to make the chapters/ topics/expressions more simplified. The teaching of simplification procedures may make the subjects more communicative.

(8) To make the core subjects like Physics, Chemistry, Mathematics, Botany,Zoology,Biotechnology,Civil Enginnering,Electrical, Electronics etc., more communicative efforts may be made by the academicians to

simplify the useful portion of the subjects for easy communication among the masses.

Conclusion

To use a language properly we have to know the grammatical structure of the language, but we should also know what forms of language are appropriate in a particular situation. There are varieties of English such as American English, British English, and Indian English either formal or informal English etc.

Since in communicative language teaching methods, communicative competence is the desired goal, this method ranks above other methods of language teaching in present day scenario. For implementing this language teachers need proper orientations in an organized manner. As proper articulation is an essential feature of a good personality, the language teachers must look into the shortcomings of the individual learners and help them in developing proper communicative skills, taking the rules of etiquette and politeness in speech into consideration.

An organization is a place where people are working at different levels. They all have their own opinions and approaches. For a common profit all the different people must join hands together. In today's world of technical advancement a lot of importance is given to effective communication skills.

The dominance of English in the administrative world is still prevalent and therefore we have to focus our attention conversation in English in India.

Hence, we can say that English is a language of Technocrats and Professionals.

Bibliography

Authors	Name of Books
1. Rao, S.S.Prabhakar	English for Professional Students
2. Wood, F.T. Publ.	Current English Usages, Macmillan
3. Sharma, S.R.	Teaching & Development of English
4. Kachru,B.B. English language in India	The Indiannisation of English,The
5. Samantary,Swati Communicative English	Business Communication and
6. Sahu, Nandini Language Teaching	Post-Modernist Delegation to English

Journal:

E.L.T. Journal by Cook,G.

IGNOU,Material-Communication Technology

News Papers:

The Times of India [Education Times]

The Hindustan Times [Competitive Edge]

Magazines:

English Today, New Delhi

British Lingua, Patna

Website:

www.prwb.com

www.4bb.com

Best Regards

DEEPESH KUMAR THAKUR

MA, MBA

+91-9654636679

Printed in Great Britain
by Amazon

19388094R00058